Lucy Kirkwood

CHIMERICA

NICK HERN BOOKS

London

www.nickhernbooks.co.uk

A Nick Hern Book

Chimerica first published in Great Britain as a paperback original in 2013 by
Nick Hern Books Limited, The Glasshouse, 49a Goldhawk Road, London
W12 8QP

Reprinted in this revised edition in 2013

Chimerica copyright © 2013 Lucy Kirkwood

Lucy Kirkwood has asserted her right to be identified as the author of this work

Cover photo: Jeff Widener / AP / Press Association Images
Cover design: Ned Hoste, 2H

Typeset by Nick Hern Books, London
Printed in Great Britain by CPI Group (UK) Ltd

A CIP catalogue record for this book is available from the British Library

ISBN   978 1 84842 350 3

CAUTION   All rights whatsoever in this play are strictly reserved. Requests
to reproduce the text in whole or in part should be addressed to the publisher.

Amateur Performing Rights   Applications for performance, including
readings and excerpts, by amateurs in the English language throughout the
world should be addressed to the Performing Rights Manager, Nick Hern
Books, The Glasshouse, 49a Goldhawk Road, London W12 8QP,
tel +44 (0)20 8749 4953, *e-mail* info@nickhernbooks.co.uk, except as follows:

Australia: Dominie Drama, 8 Cross Street, Brookvale 2100, *fax* (2) 9938 8695,
e-mail drama@dominie.com.au

New Zealand: Play Bureau, PO Box 420, New Plymouth, *fax* (6) 753 2150,
e-mail play.bureau.nz@xtra.co.nz

South Africa: DALRO (pty) Ltd, PO Box 31627, 2017 Braamfontein,
tel (11) 712 8000, fax (11) 403 9094, *e-mail* theatricals@dalro.co.za

United States and Canada: Casarotto Ramsay and Associates Ltd, see details
below

Professional Performing Rights   Applications for performance by
professionals in any medium and in any language throughout the world should
be addressed to Casarotto Ramsay and Associates Ltd, Waverley House,
7–12 Noel Street, London W1F 8GQ, *fax* +44 (0)20 7287 9128,
e-mail agents@casarotto.co.uk

No performance of any kind may be given unless a licence has been obtained.
Applications should be made before rehearsals begin. Publication of this play
does not necessarily indicate its availability for amateur performance.

MIX
Paper from
responsible sources
FSC   FSC® C013604

UNIVERSITY OF WINCHESTER

Chimerica was first performed at the Almeida Theatre, London, on 20 May 2013 and transferred to the Harold Pinter Theatre, London, on 6 August 2013. The cast was as follows:

TESSA KENDRICK	Claudie Blakley
JOE SCHOFIELD	Stephen Campbell Moore
LIULI/JENNIFER	Elizabeth Chan
MICHELLE/MARY CHANG/ DENG	Vera Chok
DAVID BARKER/PETER ROURKE/PAUL KRAMER/ OFFICER HYTE	Karl Collins
FRANK HADLEY/HERB/ DRUG DEALER	Trevor Cooper
BARB/DOREEN/MARIA DUBIECKI/KATE/JUDY	Nancy Crane
MEL STANWYCK	Sean Gilder
FENG MEIHUI/MING XIAOLI	Sarah Lam
YOUNG ZHANG LIN/BENNY	Andrew Leung
ZHANG WEI/WANG PENGSI	David K.S. Tse
ZHANG LIN	Benedict Wong

Other parts were played by the company

Director	Lyndsey Turner
Set Design	Es Devlin
Lighting	Tim Lutkin
Sound	Carolyn Downing
Video	Finn Ross
Costume Design	Christina Cunningham
Movement Director	Georgina Lamb
Casting	Julia Horan CDG
Associate Director	James Yeatman
Assistant Director	Ng Choon Ping
Dialect Coach	Michaela Kennen
Mandarin Coach	Bobby Xinyue
Fight Director	Bret Yount

From 2nd September 2013, the following cast changes took place: Wendy Kweh replaced Vera Chok, Liz Sutherland replaced Sarah Lam.

Author's Note

It is a fact there was a Tank Man. It is a fact that photographs were taken of him. Beyond that, everything that transpires in the play is an imaginative leap.

This is especially the case with the journalist at the centre of the story, who is not based in any way upon a real person, alive or dead. Nor is he an amalgam of many of them. Joe is purely a fictional construct.

One of the reasons I felt able to take this liberty was that the image of the Tank Man we are familiar with in fact exists in a number of forms in common currency. There are at least six recognised versions, the play takes place in an imagined universe in which there are seven. In reality, Jeff Widener's is the most famous, and I'm very grateful to him for allowing us to use his version in the publicity for the play. Versions of the shot were also taken by Stuart Franklin, Charlie Cole, Arthur Tsang Hin Wah and Terril Jones. Again, Joe is not a cipher for any of these men.

The sources the play draws on are too vast to list here, but special mention must be made of both Don McCullin's book *Unreasonable Behaviour*, and *When China Rules the World* by Martin Jacques, works I found myself returning to again and again over the years, along with two of Susan Sontag's works, *On Photography* and *Regarding the Pain of Others*, and the PSB documentary on the Tank Man. Niall Ferguson coined the term 'Chimerica', I read it in his book *The Ascent of Money*. In writing Ming Xiaoli I found Anchee Min's recollections in both the Taschen book of Chinese Propaganda posters and her own book, *Red Azalea*, very useful.

The play took six years to write, and accrued debts to many people in that time. I would like to thank:

Jack Bradley for commissioning me to write the play, and both he and Dawn Walton for their guidance and support in its early incarnations. Ben Power for rescuing the play when it became homeless, and for his dramaturgy and encouragement. Rupert Goold and Robert Icke whose long-term faith in the play is the reason it made it to the stage. Michael Attenborough and Lucy Morrison for embracing the play with such passion, giving it a home at the Almeida, and moving heaven and earth to ensure it had the best possible production. Es Devlin and Chiara Stephenson, whose wonderful designs greatly influenced the ideas and rhythms of the final drafts. Robin Pharaoh, whose crash course in doing business in China was invaluable. Choon Ping and Bobby Xinyue, for their insights into Chinese language and culture, and their work on the Mandarin translations. Stuart Glassborow. Ruru Li. John Bashford and the students of LAMDA. Mel Kenyon, for her tenacious support and incisive notes.

Most of all, Lyndsey Turner, for her rigorous dramaturgy, dedication, hard graft and theatrical imagination. The debt the play and I owe to her cannot be overestimated.

And always, Ed Hime.

L.K.

'Images transfix. Images anaesthetise.'

Susan Sontag

*'I believe in the power of the imagination to remake the world,
to release the truth within us, to hold back the night, to
transcend death, to charm motorways, to ingratiate ourselves
with birds, to enlist the confidences of madmen.'*

J.G. Ballard

Characters

JOE SCHOFIELD
FRANK HADLEY
MEL STANWYCK
TESSA KENDRICK
ZHANG LIN
HERB
BARB
ZHANG WEI
DOREEN
PAUL KRAMER
WAITRESS
YOUNG ZHANG LIN
LIULI
MARIA DUBIECKI
DAVID BARKER
MARY CHANG
WOMAN IN STRIP CLUB
MICHELLE
OFFICER HYTE
DRUG DEALER
JENNIFER LEE
FENG MEIHUI
PENGSI
PENGSI'S WIFE
MING XIAOLI
KATE
DENG
PETER ROURKE
DAWN
JUDY
GUARD
BENNY
NURSE

Also CROWDS, WAITRESS, AIR HOSTESS, SOLDIERS,
COUPLE IN RESTAURANT, BARMAID, GIRL IN STRIP
CLUB, CAMERAMAN, GUARDS, GALLERY ASSISTANT

Note on Text

A forward slash (/) indicates an overlap in speech.

A dash (–) indicates an abrupt interruption.

Starred dialogue indicates two or more characters speaking
simultaneously.

A comma on its own line indicates a beat.

A beat doesn't always mean a pause but can also denote a shift
in thought or energy. When lines are broken by a comma or a
line break, it's generally to convey a breath, a hesitation, a
grasping for words. Actors are welcome to ignore this.

Chinese Names

For those who do not know, it's worth noting that in Chinese
names the family or surname comes first, the given name
second. Traditionally a generation name, shared by family
members of the same generation, prefixes the given name.

So in Wang Pengfei, Wang is his surname, Peng his generation
name, which he shares with his brother, and Fei his given name.

Married women do not take their husband's surname but retain
their own.

ACT ONE

Scene One

*An image of a man with two shopping bags in a white shirt,
standing in front of a line of tanks. It is important he is
Chinese... but we cannot see this from the photograph. It is
important it was taken by an American... but we cannot know
this simply by looking at it. It is a photograph of heroism. It is a
photograph of protest. It is a photograph of one country by
another country.*

Scene Two

*5th June, 1989. A hotel room overlooking Tiananmen Square.
Split scene,* JOE SCHOFIELD (*nineteen*) *is speaking on the
landline phone with his editor,* FRANK (*forty-five*), *in the
newsroom of a New York newspaper.* JOE *has his camera slung
round his neck, watching the square below. It's around ten a.m.
for* JOE, *eleven p.m. for* FRANK.

FRANK. We're trying to get you on the ten fifteen out of Beijing
    tomorrow morning, but the airport's in chaos, the BBC might
    have a spot on their charter, did you meet Kate Adie yet?

JOE. No, I don't think so.

FRANK. She's a doll. Underneath, you sure you're not hurt?

JOE. I told you, I'm fine.

FRANK. I should never've sent you overseas, not so soon, not
    on your own, a situation like this, you need experience –

JOE. It was a student protest, didn't know it was gonna turn into
    a massacre, / did we?

FRANK. You're not even old enough to drink, chrissakes, what was I – don't go out again, okay? You stay there, in the hotel, just focus on getting those films back to us.

JOE. You gonna give me a front page, Frank?

FRANK. Yes, Joey, I think three hundred Chinese people being gunned down by their own government warrants a little more than a hundred words on page six, don't you?

JOE. It was more than that. I was down there, Frank, it was – three hundred, is that what they're saying? I don't know, but it was a lot more than –

JOE *freezes, looking out of the window.*

Oh fuck.

JOE *moves to the window, crouches down, watching the man who has walked out.*

FRANK. Joe?

JOE. Oh fuck, what is he doing? What is he – Jesus, get out of the road, you stupid –

JOE *realises the man's actions are entirely intentional.*

Oh my God.

FRANK. What's going on there? Joey, talk to me, what are you –

JOE. This guy. He has these… bags, like grocery bags and he… he just walked out in front of the tanks, and he's just standing there like – I mean, they could just run him right over. But he won't move, he *won't move*, he's, he's incredible, I wish you could…

JOE *stares, transfixed, breathless. Unconsciously copies the Tank Man's movements, as if he were holding two shopping bags.*

FRANK. Okay, Joe, don't worry, we're going to get you / out of –

JOE. Will you just shut up a second?

Frank, this guy, he's my age.

I think I'm about to watch him get shot.

Silence. JOE *picks up his camera. Starts taking pictures.*

FRANK. Well, did they do it yet?

JOE. No. Not yet. I'm gonna put down the phone for a second.

JOE lays the receiver down. Takes pictures. Suddenly, banging on the door.

(*Sotto.*) Shit.

He gently hangs up the phone.

FRANK. Joe? What's happening –

Lights down on FRANK. JOE *quickly winds his camera film to the end. Takes the film out, grabs more used films from his bag, empties dirty underwear out of a plastic bag, puts the films in, ties a tight knot. The phone rings.* JOE *makes a silent gesture at it, runs off, to the bathroom. The phone stops ringing. The banging ceases.* JOE *returns without the films. Listening. He goes to the door, puts his ear to it. Puts a new film in his camera, takes shot after shot of the carpet. Shaking with adrenaline. Gathers his camera bag, film. Pulls on his jacket. The phone rings, he dives for it, whispers:*

JOE. Frank?

Lights up on FRANK.

FRANK. Jesus, Joey, what are you trying to do to me!

JOE. There were fucking guards outside the door!

FRANK. Well, are they gone? Are you okay?

JOE. Yeah! My heart's fucking, like, you know?

FRANK. Yeah, what about your films?

JOE. I put them in the toilet cistern –

FRANK. Good boy. You get a good frame of that guy?

JOE. I don't know, I was just spraying and praying, listen, Frank, I'll call you back –

FRANK. You will not call me back, you stay on this line, / you hear me!

JOE. Frank, I lost him, I / have to –

FRANK. What d'you mean, you lost him?

JOE. I mean I can't see him any more, I have to go down there, see if I can –

The door smashes open. A swarm of CHINESE SOLDIERS enter. JOE drops the phone, stands, puts his hands up, backs away.

FRANK. Joe? JOEY!

Lights down on FRANK as the SOLDIERS shout at JOE in Mandarin. JOE remains frozen with his hands up as one SOLDIER steadily aims at him while another grabs his camera, takes the film out, throws the camera against the wall. Punches JOE in the stomach, JOE sinks to the floor. Chaos, violence, shouts in Chinese dialects as we travel forward twenty-three years to…

Scene Three

A plane. JOE is forty-two years old. MEL STANWYCK (forty-five) to his right, TESSA KENDRICK (English) to his left, reading a magazine, knocking back a cocktail. JOE and MEL have beers.

MEL. It's a seven-star hotel, Joe. Why wouldn't you want to stay in a seven-star hotel?

JOE. I told you –

MEL. The website says it has an 'auspicious garden'. An auspicious garden, Joe.

JOE. Yeah but I haven't seen Zhang Lin / for –

MEL. Sure, right, your friend.

An AIR HOSTESS enters. TESS speaks quietly to her, she takes TESS's empty glass and goes.

JOE. First time I went back to Beijing, Mel, I was so green
you wouldn't believe it, Zhang Lin asks to meet me, offers
to teach me Mandarin, he bought me a *suit* – I ever tell you
that, he bought me a fucking Armani suit! We only have
two days, I just want to hang out with him a little. And
Frank won't sign off your expenses, staying in a place
like that.

JOE *shows* MEL *some photographs on his phone.*

MEL. Ah, I'm gonna haggle them down. I gotta spend two days
in a Chinese plastics factory, I want a seven-star mini-bar to
fall asleep with. (*Re: the photos.*) What's this?

JOE. Somalia.

MEL. You see Greg out there?

JOE. You didn't hear?

MEL. Dead?

JOE. Only from the waist down. Thirteen-year-old sniper.

MEL. Man, that sucks. I have to find a new racquetball partner.

PILOT (*voice-over*). Welcome to Flight 9012 from New York
JFK to Beijing, approximate landing time in fifteen hours.

MEL *hands the phone back. The* HOSTESS *brings* TESS *a
fresh drink.*

MEL (*sotto*). You know, that's her third since we sat down?

JOE (*looks, shrugs*). Complimentary, isn't it?

MEL. I'm just saying, fifteen hours next to Zelda Fitzgerald,
could be a bumpy ride.

TESS *looks at them.* MEL *immediately grins, friendly, raises
his beer.*

Cheers!

TESS *looks back down at her magazine.*

TESS. A pansy with hair on his chest.

JOE. Excuse me?

TESS (*turns a page*). That's how Zelda Fitzgerald described Hemingway.

Pause. JOE *and* MEL *look at each other.*

MEL. Switch seats with me.

JOE. No. (*To* TESS.) So is this your first time in Beijing?

She looks up from the magazine. Smiles.

TESS. Yes.

She looks back down at the magazine. MEL *leans across* JOE.

MEL. Business? Pleasure?

TESS (*still reading*). Are you asking or offering?

MEL. Oh, honey, I'm a recently divorced journalist, I'm no good for either, hey listen, I got a tip for you: *don't eat the chicken.*

JOE. Don't listen to – you can eat the chicken, the chicken / is fine –

MEL. The average piece of Chinese chicken, if you were an athlete, and you ate this chicken, I tell you the steroids they pump into that shit, you would fail a doping test.

JOE. Don't freak her out.

MEL. True story.

JOE. You speak Mandarin?

MEL. And don't eat the beef either, 'less you're sure that's what it is.

TESS sighs, closes her magazine.

TESS. I can read it a bit.

MEL. They have this *paint*, okay, they paint the chicken, so it looks like beef, but it ain't beef. It's the Lance Armstrong of the poultry world.

JOE. Mel, tell her about the place.

MEL. What place?

JOE. The place, our place, with the *bāozi* and the asshole waiter.

MEL. Oh my God, yeah, okay, you have to go to this
    restaurant –

JOE. Write it down for her.

MEL. I'll write it down for you, you like spicy food?

TESS. I have an asbestos mouth.

    '

JOE. So what are you working on out there?

TESSA. I can't really say.

JOE. No, sure but?

    '

    JOE *and* MEL *look at her, expectant.*

TESS. I categorise people. By, well, anything, purchasing
    habits, political affiliations, sexual politics. I'm refining the
    profiling system that… this company uses, we have a
    Western model but it has to be adapted to the Chinese
    market.

JOE. So I'm not the special little snowflake my mom always
    told me I was?

TESS. Sorry to be the one to break it to you. No such thing as
    an individual.

MEL. Sure, well, maybe not in China, man, I hate this shit.

TESS. Excuse me?

MEL. This 'if you picked mostly As, you're a summer-wedding
    kind of girl!' *scheisse*, this insistence people are some…
    bovine breed, self-selecting themselves into bullshit
    constellations, tell me what my *future* is off the back of
    whether I take sugar or sweetener in my coffee. I know
    Democrats who play golf with Donald Trump, I've met dirt-
    poor Polish guys who can recite the works of Walt Whitman
    by heart, millionaires who don't know how to hold a fucking
    fish knife, you're going to a country of one *billion* people to
    make some nice boxes to put them in?

TESS *stares at him. Drains her drink.*

TESS. Okay, I've had, like, four of these now, but I'd say, let's see, I'd say you're probably a… Group O, with Group B characteristics.

MEL. Group O, Group O, I mean, what a *sad*, what a really *prosaic* way to view / your fellow humans!

TESS. Within that, I'd place you as an Anti-Materialist. At some point you were probably Urban Cool with a bit of Bright Young Thing, but I think that ship has sailed, don't you? You see your work as a career rather than a job, you identify yourself as international rather than national, you have no brand loyalty, your favourite movie is *Goodfellas*, you believe cannabis should be legalised, that contraception is a woman's responsibility, that little can be done to change life, that children should eat what they're given, and that real men don't cry.

'

I'm sorry, that's quite a limited, I'd need to ask a few more questions.

JOE. She's a witch.

MEL. No, okay, because okay a) that thing about the contraception is just plain wrong, because *I* had a vasectomy, b) *Goodfellas* isn't even in my top ten.

TESS. *Singin' in the Rain*?

MEL (*takes out his book*). I want to read now.

TESS. I know, it's awful, isn't it? No one likes to know to they're unremarkable. (*To the* HOSTESS, *her glass*.)'Scuse me? When you get a sec? Cheers.

JOE. You gonna do me now?

TESS. I'm not a machine.

PILOT (*voice-over*). Ladies and gentlemen, we are now approaching take-off. The time is eight fifty-two p.m. local time and the skies are clear.

The plane starts take-off. TESS *shuts her eyes.*

TESS (*sotto*). Oh, shit. Oh, shit.

JOE (*grins*). What's the matter? It's only China, coming towards you at five hundred miles an hour.

TESS. Stop it!

JOE. Are you okay?

TESS. No. No, I'm scared we're going to crash and die.

JOE. Take-off's the worst. You'll be okay once we get in the air.

MEL. You know why they tell you to adopt the brace position? So your teeth don't smash and they can identify your body by your dental records.

JOE. Mel! Leave her alone, she's scared.

MEL. Aren't we all, sweetheart. Aren't we all, listen to this: '"I like to kiss very much," she said. "But I do not do it well."'

JOE *takes* TESS*'s hand*.

JOE. Hi. I'm Joe Schofield.

TESS. Tessa Kendrick.

MEL (*looking at the book cover*). This guy. This fucking guy.

JOE *and* TESS *look at each other as the plane soars into the sky*.

Scene Four

Tiananmen Square. A huge image of Mao. JOE *shakes* ZHANG LIN*'s hand*.

JOE. So you haven't changed one bit.

ZHANG LIN. No, I have two more inches here – (*His stomach.*) It's rude of you not to notice.

JOE. That's the hotel I was staying in, over there. I can see my window –

ZHANG LIN. Yes, yes, I know, you told me. Fifteen up, four across, it's strange they haven't renamed it after you yet. Have you eaten?

JOE (*makes a face*). Factory cafeteria food.

ZHANG LIN. Right, your trip. Did it go well?

JOE. Terrifying. You ever been to one of those places?

ZHANG LIN. My brother's a foreman in a factory, just outside Beijing.

JOE. Mel spoke with these women, they were earning like fifty dollars a month, working fifteen-hour days, sleeping on the floor –

ZHANG LIN. Zhang Wei started like that. The one he works in now, it's much better. He earns a thousand dollars a month. His son's been studying at Harvard.

JOE. I just, I felt so guilty –

ZHANG LIN. Yes, you're right, we all blame you too. I think I read a book once, about the *Mayflower*, crossing the Atlantic. Apparently this was quite terrifying also. You've heard of this ship?

JOE. Yes, Zhang Lin, I have heard of the *Mayflower*. But they're not travelling to a whole new country –

ZHANG LIN. Of course they are. It just occupies the same part of the atlas as the old one.

,

JOE. You should've been a lawyer, you know that?

ZHANG LIN. I like teaching. I teach Crazy English now, did I tell you?

JOE. Yeah, you said, I thought it was like a metaphor or –

ZHANG LIN. No! I take my students to the roof, we yell English into the sky. You shout, you learn. Conquer English to make China stronger! It's got a sort of fascist aspect but it helps with conjugation. You look tired, Joe.

JOE. Thanks.

HERB, *an American tourist from Boston, approaches* JOE, *spying a white face.*

HERB. 'Scuse me, you're American, right?

JOE. *Désolé, monsieur, je ne peux pas vous aider.*

ZHANG LIN. Joe, behave yourself. My friend is having a joke with you, sir.

HERB. Huh. So I was wondering if you could take picture of me and my wife?

BARBARA *comes over.* HERB *puts his arm round her. Passes his camera to* JOE.

ZHANG LIN. You're honoured. This man is one of the world's finest photographers.

HERB. Barb, you hear that? You famous?

JOE. No, / Zhang Lin, don't –

HERB. No, I mean you in galleries?

JOE. You ever heard of the Museum of Modern Art?

HERB. Sure. Sure I have –

JOE. Well, sir, they never heard of me. You want to shuffle in a little bit?

HERB *and* BARBARA *shuffle closer to each other.*

HERB. Barb's a history nut. She wanted to see Tiananmen Square. Right, hon?

BARBARA. I like to expand my horizons. Pull in your gut Herb.

HERB *sucks in as* JOE *takes the picture.* JOE *grins. Hands the camera back.*

JOE. You guys have a good trip now.

The tourists go. JOE *takes up his camera, turns back towards the hotel, taking pictures.* ZHANG LIN *looks, nervous, at a casually dressed* MAN *holding an umbrella as he wanders closer.*

ZHANG LIN. Joe.

JOE. Can't believe they haven't pulled it down yet. Every time I come back, I get surprised it's still here.

ZHANG LIN. Joe, put your camera away.

JOE goes to take a picture. The MAN *opens his umbrella in front of* JOE, *obscuring his shot.* JOE *looks at* ZHANG LIN. *Understands. He puts his camera down.*

You want to drop your bag at the apartment, get a beer?

JOE. Sure.

ZHANG LIN. My brother is coming round. He wants to buy us dinner.

Lights up on ZHANG LIN*'s apartment.* ZHANG LIN *and* JOE *with beers. They've been drinking a while, and are muffled against the cold. Every time* ZHANG LIN *takes a sip of his beer, he clinks his bottle with* JOE*'s.* JOE *stands, acting out the scenario he describes.*

JOE. So okay I'm standing there, my editor's on the phone having a fucking conniption, and the Tank Man just walks out, he just walks right out, and my heart is / just –

ZHANG LIN. I know, you said, then the guards come, and you put the films in the toilet / cistern –

JOE. Right, and then he's just… gone, he's just. This guy. Zhang Lin, this fucking guy, I can't, I still can't… because how does a guy like that just disappear? To come out of a massacre, to have the fucking wherewithal to, to, to stand up, to say this is wrong. This is wrong and, and someone has to say so.

He is lost in thought, captivated by his memory for a moment.

ZHANG LIN. Didn't you meet Nelson Mandela?

JOE. People always say that but, it's a politician's job to stick his head over the parapet, they have a whole fucking machine around them, what did the Tank Man have? Nothing. Plastic grocery bags, is all.

ZHANG LIN. And you only have a camera.

JOE. Sure, and in twenty-three years I never did a thing that came close to half a minute of that man's life. Ah, shut up, Joe.

,

You know, you should come to the States.

ZHANG LIN *laughs*.

I'm serious.

ZHANG LIN. It's not possible.

JOE. Sure it is. Cos of the green card you mean? Listen, you know how many Upper East Side assholes want their spawn speaking Mandarin? You could clean up.

ZHANG LIN. Clean up what? Public bathrooms?

JOE. Very funny. I mean it, you should come to New York.

ZHANG LIN. What for? Starbucks? Cockroaches? I can get both of those here.

JOE. Sure, and Walmart and McDonald's, / I know, it's turning into America, but –

ZHANG LIN. You have Walmart. Why are we not allowed Walmart?

JOE. Only with none of the good parts, don't you want those things?

ZHANG LIN. Things here are okay. Better. You know how much has changed, how fast?

JOE. Sure, but seriously, this country –

ZHANG LIN. This country owns you. You don't get to lecture us any more. I subscribe to this website, for my teaching, it sends me new American slangs and phrases each week. You know what phrase I learnt this week? Fiscal cliff.

JOE. I just, I remember being here in 1989 and there was hope, on the streets, in the square, people, like… imagining a, a, a future or whatever / and where has that –

ZHANG LIN. I don't want to talk about this.

JOE. Yeah I know, only I saw it too –

ZHANG LIN. Yes, up in your hotel room, taking pictures.
Behind your camera, plane ticket in your pocket, I was there.
Down there, in the square, bullets the size of your thumb,
yes? Dumdums, they open up inside you. They turned the
lights out on us –

JOE. Zhang Lin –

ZHANG LIN. They turned the lights out to scare us and then... I
don't know. Maybe they did not come back on again for me.

  ZHANG LIN *holds up his empty bottle.*

  Shall we have another?

  ZHANG LIN *takes another beer from the fridge. Searches
  for the opener.*

JOE. I'm sorry. It's just. I don't know, you type Tiananmen
Square into a search engine here, you get three pages from
the Tourist Board, the Tank Man is dead in more ways than
one, and what for?

ZHANG LIN. The Tank Man? What are you – you want to
reduce this to one man? There were a hundred-thousand of
us, Joe, we're not dead! We just made some choices you
don't approve of! Have you seen the opener? I can't –
anyway, who told you that?

JOE. What?

ZHANG LIN. Who told you the Tank Man was dead?

JOE. I don't know. I just assumed... sorry, what are you – ?

ZHANG LIN (*searching*). Things have feet in this apartment.

JOE. So where is he?

ZHANG LIN. I don't know.

JOE. No but what are you saying?

ZHANG LIN. Nothing. I've been drinking all afternoon, I
shouldn't have.

ZHANG LIN *gives up searching. Tries to take the cap off with his teeth.*

JOE. Shouldn't have what?

Don't do that – you'll break a tooth.

ZHANG LIN (*laughs*). You can't handle the tooth!

JOE. Are you saying he's / still alive?

ZHANG LIN. You know this movie?

JOE. But, but is that what you're saying?

ZHANG LIN. Jack Nicholson, / it's pretty good –

JOE. Oh my God. Oh my God, is he alive? Zhang Lin, please, you have to –

ZHANG LIN. It was twenty-three years ago.

JOE. Yes or no?

ZHANG LIN. Joe.

JOE. Yes or no?

,

ZHANG LIN. He went to America, I believe. New York, probably. Many of the organisers went to New York. After. By August, most of my friends were gone.

JOE. You never mentioned this before.

ZHANG LIN. You never asked.

JOE. Did you know him?

ZHANG LIN. No. Not well.

JOE. But – so you know his name?

ZHANG LIN. What does it matter? You know he probably *is* dead, he probably went to America and got hit by a Cadillac on Route 66.

JOE. Do you know his name?

ZHANG LIN. Or his heart exploded, from all the beef.

JOE. What is his name?

ZHANG LIN. He'll have changed it. He'll be called Brian
  Simpson / or –

JOE. So just tell me. Please.

  ,

ZHANG LIN. I think it was Wang Pengfei.

JOE. Wang Pengfei?

  ,

ZHANG LIN. Anyway, don't you have other things to worry
  about? Your country, it's – what's the word? Fucked?

  ,

JOE. Okay: you can have my vote. Seeing as how you don't
  care about getting your own. You pick my candidate and I'll
  vote for them.

ZHANG LIN. Okay. I like Clinton.

JOE. Okay, well you're four years late for that. Or four years
  early, I don't know, she just resigned. You got two choices,
  Obama or Romney.

ZHANG LIN. Romney hates the Chinese. I like Clinton.

JOE. Why?

ZHANG WEI (*off, Mandarin*). Is he here? Is he here?

ZHANG LIN. Women hold up half the sky.

  ZHANG WEI *enters, with two shopping bags. He wears
  neon Nikes, is delighted to see* JOE.

ZHANG WEI (*Mandarin*). He's here!

  ZHANG WEI *dumps his bags. Shakes* JOE*'s hand
  enthusiastically.*

ZHANG LIN. This is my brother, Zhang Wei. (*Mandarin.*) This
  is Joe. He just gave me his vote.

ZHANG WEI (*Mandarin*). An election every four years. No
  wonder they can't get anything done.

ZHANG LIN. He speaks Mandarin.

JOE (*halting Mandarin*). Not very well.

ZHANG WEI (*English*). My boy. My boy Benny. Harvard University.

He gestures to ZHANG LIN, *'tell him'*.

ZHANG LIN. My nephew, he just graduated from Harvard. Very smart kid. He's about to move to New York, we'd appreciate it if you looked him up.

JOE. Sure, I'll do that.

ZHANG WEI. My shoes, tell him about my shoes, Dog-face.

ZHANG LIN. He bought Zhang Wei those ugly shoes.

JOE. Very nice, what did he call you? Just then, he called you dog... something –

ZHANG LIN. Oh. Dog-face, yes. It's a family name. When babies are small, we give them a milk name, words that make them sound disgusting. To stop the King of Hell stealing them away. Mine got stuck to me. Let's eat.

JOE. Where are we going?

ZHANG LIN. Somewhere very special, I've been saving up, it's called 'the Pizza Hut'.

JOE. Oh. Sure. Great. I just need to make a call.

Beat. Then ZHANG LIN *cracks up. To* ZHANG WEI, *in Mandarin*.

ZHANG LIN. Did you see his face!

ZHANG WEI. What did you say?

ZHANG LIN. I told him we were going to Pizza Hut!

ZHANG WEI *laughs. Gestures to one of his bags, which contains a spare pair of shoes.*

ZHANG WEI. Just let me change my shoes.

Scene Five

Lights up on FRANK *in his Manhattan corner office, with* JOE *and* MEL. *He is the editor of a major American newspaper. In his late fifties, beautifully dressed. A large, impressive desk.*

FRANK. The Tank Man is dead, you don't think your friend is, let's be civil about this, you don't think he's maybe you know feeding you a crock / of –

JOE. No, but look at how it actually happened:

DOREEN, FRANK*'s PA enters.* JOE *positions two chairs and a pot plant to represent the tanks.*

Okay so here, these are the tanks, and this… (*Looks around, sees* DOREEN.) Doreen, can I grab you for a second? Thanks, okay, so – yeah, hold those, that's great, so Doreen is the Tank Man. And she's, he's holding his ground…

JOE *hands her* FRANK's *briefcase and a backpack to represent the Tank Man's shopping bags.*

Then this guy on a bicycle comes gliding out. Mel, you wanna –

MEL *acts the man on the bicycle. He does a jerky circling motion with his right leg.*

What the hell are you doing?

MEL. I'm on a bicycle!

JOE. Then there's a couple other guys – (*Points to himself.*) They motion him, they guide him… into the crowd… and he disappears.

JOE *guides* DOREEN *behind a drape. She disappears. Beat.* JOE *looks to* FRANK. *Ta-dah.*

FRANK. Into the arms of the Public Security Bureau where he's shot at point-blank range in the head and thrown in an unmarked mass grave.

JOE. No, but the PSB, they're violent, you know? They bend your arm back, they rough you up. I don't know. The bicycle, the way they… guided him. It was gentle.

DOREEN (*from behind drape*). Are we done here?

JOE. Sure. Thanks, Doreen.

DOREEN *comes out from behind the drape. Puts the file on* FRANK'*s desk.*

DOREEN. I need you to sign these off.

FRANK. Can it wait? I'm kind of in the middle of… (*To* JOE.) just, give me a minute, okay?

FRANK *quickly opens the file, zips through the couple of contact sheets within.*

No… no… definitely not… maybe this one if you crop it, give me a pen –

DOREEN *hands him a pen, he circles the shot.* JOE'*s eye is caught, he moves closer to the desk.*

JOE. What's this? Are these mine?

FRANK. We can't use this. / (*To* DOREEN.) See if Dina got anything we can go with.

JOE. Frank, that's my only war story all year, this is two weeks' work, why can't you –

FRANK *picks up his cup of coffee and takes a gulp.*

FRANK. Don't play the ingénue with me, you know why, this is not the first time we have had this conversation, they are, without exception, ghoulish. / (This is cold. Doreen? This is cold.)

He hands DOREEN *the cup. She exits.* MEL *rests his feet against* FRANK'*s desk.*

JOE. If it bleeds, it leads. That's what you said to me. First day on the job that's what you said to me, what about this one?

FRANK. No faces. (*To* MEL.) Feet.

MEL *takes his feet off the woodwork.*

JOE. It's a corpse you can hardly see / his –

FRANK. *No faces.* (*Hollering off.*) / Doreen? Coffee? Thank you!

MEL. Leave it, Joe. Butter him up, you said, not / nail his balls to the wall.

FRANK. And my pill, I forgot to take my pill! Why am I being buttered?

DOREEN *comes in with a cup of coffee and a pill.* FRANK *takes the pill. As* DOREEN *leaves:*

DOREEN. You have a meeting with the lawyers at ten.

JOE. So, okay. We were thinking, we do a special. On China. Its history, its future. The centrepiece is a shot of the Tank Man, sitting in Central Park. Alive and well.

FRANK. And where do I put this special?

JOE. In the magazine.

FRANK. That's not really the kind of story sits well / in the –

JOE. It used to be.

FRANK. And I used to have a prostate, shit happens. Lifestyle and leisure, that's the magazine's remit, and this is hypothetical anyway. It's a great idea, boys, I can see why you're excited, but I don't have the money for this.

JOE. You don't have money for one of the great heroes in twentieth-century history?

FRANK. I don't even have the money for our food critic to review anywhere you don't BYOB. Our revenues are down eleven per cent, what am I supposed to do, keep you on payroll, file your expenses, while the pair of you gallivant round the / city –

MEL. 'Gallivant'?

FRANK. Gallivant, jaunt, roam the fucking city in the middle of an election, looking for a man who may or may not still be alive who most likely isn't too excited about having years of anonymity blown by two self-serving newsmen looking to make a scoop.

JOE. You're not interested in China?

FRANK. You know, this dime-store rhetoric is not flattering to you. I *am* interested in China, because I am not a fucking idiot. I just *sent* you to China, didn't I?

JOE. Okay, so why can't we –

FRANK. Because that's not a story about China, that's about America; American jobs, American money, and right now, unless you can give me an angle like that on the Tank Man, I can't let you pursue it, not in the middle of campaign season.

MEL. Okay, so what about this: we take a whole 'God Bless America', 'land of the free home of the et cetera' angle on this, just a balls-out good news story. Cos they're opening their newspapers every day, and it's real wrist-slitting stuff, our national industry getting screwed over by China undercutting them at every turn –

FRANK (*guarded*). Okay, so this is interesting.

MEL. Right, because, because, okay this is what it is, because this man, strike that, this *hero*, brave, noble, persecuted, he escapes from this supposedly superior country, and where does he go? Not London, not Mumbai, not Moscow. He comes to New York. To the States. Because so what if our economy's stalling, our power is ebbing, one thing won't change: America means freedom, it means rights, set down in a constitution, to speak, to protest, to be an *individual*, it is, and will always be, the homeland of heroes.

'

FRANK. See, that wasn't so hard, was it?

MEL. Is that a green light?

DOREEN *enters with a computer printout. Hands it to* FRANK, *he doesn't look at it.*

FRANK. Don't get too excited. I still want you guys in Denver for the first debate, and you still have to find one Chinese guy in a city of – how many Chinese guys, Doreen?

DOREEN. Three hundred thousand. Give or take.

MEL. We got a name, right, Joe?

JOE. Wang Pengfei.

DOREEN. And he's dead.

,

I searched the archive. This is by Paul Kramer, he was our Beijing correspondent at the time, the headline is quite unequivocal.

FRANK. It can't be *quite* unequivocal, Doreen, it is or it isn't unequivocal, there is no scale.

DOREEN. I accessed the New York and the London *Times* too. They're all in agreement.

,

FRANK. Well. Okay. Thanks, Doreen, that… simplifies things a little.

DOREEN (*shrugs*). I mean it was right there, you only have to type it / in –

FRANK. Yep, let's just, leave the boys with a little dignity, shall we?

DOREEN *leaves, grumbling, sotto. A pause.*

Go to Colorado. There will be other Tank Men.

MEL. But –

FRANK. Mel, don't you have a deadline?

MEL *goes.* JOE *turns to follow him.* FRANK *rubs his eyes.*

Just a minute – Joe? You never think… you're what, like forty? You never think it might be / time to –

JOE. This? Again?

FRANK. – settle down. Put down some roots. I mean, you don't even have a car!

JOE. I live in New York, why do I need a / car –

FRANK. I don't know. So you'll have somewhere to sleep when I fire you, why does anyone have a car? It's freedom.

JOE (*smiles*). You know, there are these three new phrases they just started using in China: *Fang nu. Che nu. Hai nu.* Car slave. House slave. Child slave.

Pause. DOREEN *enters*.

FRANK. You are a very bleak man, anyone ever tell you that? Look, I'm not saying, but there's something to be said for – starting something. Raising a family, some nurse hands you a bundle of, whatever, right there that's, that's *growth*, that's hope in your hands. Watching your kids sleep, wiping the shit from their mouths, taking care of something that's a, it is, it's a… it's a wonderful thing. Y'know?

JOE. Yeah. You're right. Your au pair was a very lucky woman.
,

FRANK. The Tank Man. It's probably for the best. I once spent two months chasing Bob Dylan round Europe for an interview. Closest I got was a flash of sheepskin in Kraków airport. Hippies and heroes, slippery fuckers.

JOE. Never knew you were a Dylan fan, Frank.

FRANK. Only the electric stuff.

JOE *goes*. FRANK *turns to* DOREEN.

I'm sorry about before. It was impolite of me to correct you like that.

DOREEN *surveys him, inscrutable*. FRANK *looks at his coffee*.

You spat in this, didn't you?

DOREEN. You have Senator Collins on line four.

Scene Six

JOE *sits with* PAUL KRAMER *in Prospect Park, Brooklyn. A pram, a baby crying inside.* PAUL *softly rocks the pram.*

PAUL. The *Herald*? I haven't worked there for twenty years – (*To the baby.*) Good girl.

JOE. I know. But you were their Beijing correspondent in 1989, right? I found this in the archive, / 'Tank Man Executed' –

As JOE *shows him a printout,* PAUL *picks up a soft toy, dances it at the child in the pram.*

PAUL. Shhh… sweetie… look at Mr Biggins! Look at him! Look at him! Look at him! Look at him! Look at him! Look at him!

,

Look / at him –

JOE. Shall I get us a coffee?

PAUL. We don't have much time. We have a play date at twelve. Let me see that.

He puts his hand out of the pram. Pulls it back. Wipes his hand on his trousers. Grins at JOE.

'I measure my life in baby puke.'

PAUL *takes the article and scans it. The baby gurgles contentedly.*

Yeah, I didn't write this.

JOE. That's your name right there. Paul Kramer.

PAUL. I know. I can read. I didn't write this.

JOE. And you can be sure of that?

PAUL. There are two split infinitives here.

JOE. So someone else wrote it and put your name on it? Was that common?

PAUL. Sure. I was their man out in Beijing. You have a story like this, it looks better if it's written by the correspondent.

JOE. So who was it written by?

PAUL. Some news monkey. Happens all the time. Used to, anyway, you take a trip out of town, go to the dentist or whatever, doesn't matter who's covering you, the sub will stick your name on what they wrote. Looks better that way.

JOE. You never thought about this before?

PAUL. I never saw it before. I was out there. I didn't read the thing, I just wrote for it.

JOE. So if you didn't write this…

PAUL. Do I think it's true?

,

I don't know. After Tiananmen, that whole summer – they were arresting people all over the place. There were public executions on the TV every day, people who'd embarrassed the government a hell of a lot less than this guy.

JOE. So he had to have been executed, right?

PAUL. No, that's not what I'm – hey hey hey no. No! Emily don't chew that, come on –

He reaches into the pram, pulls something free of baby teeth.

(*Proud.*) She's a biter. She already has three teeth. You got any?

JOE. Teeth?

PAUL. Kids.

JOE. No.

PAUL. I'm sorry.

JOE. That's okay.

PAUL. Look, you have to think about the psychology of the thing. It's a gibbet society. They like to make examples. You don't roll a load of tanks into a public square and start firing just for the hell of it, you know? You do it to scare the hell out of people, scare them out of ever trying anything like that again. But you don't make an example if no one's watching. If the PSB had him they'd make damn sure every TV viewer in China *saw* when that bullet went into his skull. And I watched a lot of TV. And I never saw that.

But that's just my opinion.

JOE. No, thank you.

PAUL. No problem. This is for a story?

JOE. I'm trying to find him.

PAUL. Who?

JOE. The Tank Man.

PAUL (*laughs*). Right.

He sees JOE *is serious*.

Oh, okay, well. Good luck with that. I'm gonna have to go change this one.

JOE. No problem. Thanks for your time.

PAUL *exits, pushing the pram.* JOE *takes out his cellphone, dials*.

It's me. Put down the burrito, Mel.

,

Lucky guess, brush your teeth. I'm coming over.

Scene Seven

A Chinese restaurant in Manhattan. TESS *and* JOE *at a table in the dining area. A Chinese couple sit behind them, waiting for carry-out. Young and in love.*

TESS. So he's not dead?

JOE. Not according to Paul Kramer.

TESS. So that place you told me about, the restaurant in Beijing? It's gone.

JOE. What? No way, I love that place. Maybe you just got / lost or –

TESS. They built a car park on it. I was starving, I ended up in a KFC, there were all these people taking business dinners in there.

JOE. God, tell me about it, it's so depressing. Beijing's so Westernised.

TESS. I don't think so.

JOE. You kidding me? You flew seven thousand miles, had fried chicken for dinner.

TESS. No I didn't. I had a tree fungus salad and shrimp rice.

A WAITRESS *brings their food.* TESS *looks over it.*

(*Mandarin.*) Excuse me, we ordered some lotus root? *Xie xie.*

,

I totally did that to show off to you, so you better be impressed.

JOE. I am. I mean, your accent's terrible, but – no, that's. You're a fast learner huh?

TESS. I've been studying every night since I got back from Beijing. I've been taking a lot of caffeine pills. My piss is orange. I have to admit something terrible.

JOE. Worse than your piss being orange?

TESS. I googled you.

JOE. I googled you too.

TESS. Why?

JOE. Why d'you think? What's 'netball', and why do they make you wear such short skirts to play it?

,

TESS. Joe, this isn't a date. This is really just a, it's a professional thing – I was just looking at your work to, the company I'm working for, it's a credit card and we want an image, to print on it and I, I thought you might be our man and.

JOE. No, sure, don't worry about it.

TESS. It's really awkward now, isn't it?

JOE. No, not at all.

TESS. I don't think it helps to pretend it's not. Why did you think it was a date?

JOE. Why d'you *think* I thought it was a date?

'

TESS. The plane?

JOE. Yes the plane.

TESS. Oh, wow. I mean, no, but it's not exactly. I mean what would we tell our kids?

JOE. Well, I don't want kids so there's no universe in which that'd be a problem.

TESS. No, I wasn't, they're rhetorical kids, I was just. I'm sorry, I should've –

JOE. Like I said, don't worry about it.

Pause. TESS *takes out a folder. A printout from the folder. Slides it over to* JOE.

TESS. So this is the image we'd like to use. And this is the offer we're prepared to make:

She writes a number on a napkin, slides it over. JOE *doesn't look at it.*

JOE. What the hell are you doing, I feel like I'm in a high-school play or something.

TESS. This would be a good thing for you.

JOE. Well thanks, but you can't have it.

TESS. Why not?

JOE. For a fucking credit card? Why d'you think?

TESS. Don't you want to know how many zeroes there are?

JOE. That river, those kids are fishing in? It's one of the most polluted rivers in the world, the rate of childhood mortality in that village is –

TESS. It's a great image.

JOE. Sure, only there's a fucking ceiling on how much money I want to make from a bunch of kids dying in a developing country, okay?

A beat. Trying to lighten the mood:

TESS. So you'd be okay with giving it to us for free, then?

JOE *stares at her. The* WAITRESS *brings the lotus root, goes.* JOE *dishes out food. They eat in silence. Presently:*

Can I ask about your Tiananmen pictures?

JOE. You have to be fucking kidding me.

,

TESS. Oh God no, I *wouldn't* – bloody hell, it was a massacre, Joe. I'm not going to put it on a fucking credit card, nobody would – I just, I can't believe you took that.

JOE (*shrugs*). There's like six other guys got that same shot. I was just lucky I had a hotel room window in the right place.

TESS. God, you must've been a baby, I had it on my wall when I was a student. Next to Che Guevara and The Stone Roses.

JOE. Uh-uh.

They eat in silence. Until:

TESS. Do you really not know what netball is? / I mean –

JOE. No, I know what it is. It's a very slow, boring version of basketball.

TESS. Well, I think you'll find actually, when it's played at a high level –

JOE. Can you pass the soy?

,

TESS. You're really angry, aren't you?

JOE. Not at all.

TESS. Because I slept with you once and came here without intending to do it again?

JOE. No, because I missed a chance to do my laundry to have dinner with Ayn Rand. And because actually, bull*shit* you didn't have that intention –

JOE *takes his iPhone out, scrolls through it. Finds the email he is looking for.*

TESS. I think I was pretty clear in my –

JOE. 'Dear Joe, can I buy you dinner? I promise not to have sex with you.'

TESS. I'm not sure how I could have been more explicit.

JOE. Are you fucking kidding me? That's the least subtle email I ever got in my whole life!

TESS. Oh God, yes! Grant me the privilege of being the next woman Joe Schofield resents having to go home to!

JOE. Sweetheart, I've resented far better women than you.

TESS. Well, you seemed quite fond of me when your arse was banging against the hand dryer of a 747.

JOE. Hey, listen, that was an act of charity, I've been cavity-searched on the border of Russia, it was more fun.

TESS. You are so full of shit.

JOE. I don't have to like someone to have sex with them. You were scared, I just met you, what am I gonna do, assassinate your character at thirty-thousand feet?

TESS. Mel gave it his best shot.

JOE. Yeah well, Mel's an asshole.

TESS. Yeah well, at least he's honest about that –

JOE. You know, I have better things to do / than –

TESS. Oh yes, like what? Hunting the human thimble?

JOE stands, pulls on his coat, his scarf.

Yes, please, do just walk away in the middle of a – no, that's, that's really mature. We should do this again some time.

JOE tosses down money, leaves. The WAITRESS *comes, takes the money. Stares at* TESS.

He started it.

WAITRESS. We need this table. More people.

Scene Eight

ZHANG LIN*'s apartment.* ZHANG LIN *drinks beer. The TV on.* ZHANG WEI *gestures to the TV.*

ZHANG WEI (*Mandarin*). Turn it off.

ZHANG LIN (*Mandarin*). What do you want?

ZHANG WEI (*Mandarin*). I want to talk to you.

ZHANG LIN (*Mandarin*). Just let me finish this.

ZHANG WEI. Turn it off.

ZHANG LIN. I'm relaxing.

ZHANG WEI. You couldn't let me pay for dinner? You couldn't let me have that?

ZHANG LIN. He wanted to. I was too tired for an argument.

ZHANG WEI. I invited *him*. Doesn't he know anything? Anyway that's it, isn't it? That's a big opportunity wasted, completely wasted –

ZHANG LIN. You don't need to do all that with Joe, he'll look after Benny anyway.

ZHANG WEI. Makes me look presumptuous, though, doesn't it? A man like that, why should he bother with Benny?

ZHANG LIN. Because I asked him to. I've done enough for him over the years. He knows that.

ZHANG WEI. It's alright for you, you've got connections –

ZHANG LIN. What connections?

ZHANG WEI. Teaching officials and their fat-arsed kids how to speak American! But I / don't –

ZHANG LIN. I taught your fat-arsed kid too –

ZHANG WEI. I told you, you don't talk about Benny like that, okay!

ZHANG LIN. What? It's good to be fat, he's strong.

ZHANG WEI. Anyway, he's got some trainer now he's in the States, makes him run round the park with weights tied to his ankles, look at this, he looks like Huang Xiaoming –

ZHANG WEI *takes out a picture from his wallet, shows* ZHANG LIN, *proud. On the other side of the wall,* MING XIAOLI *starts to cough.*

ZHANG LIN. Maybe if Huang Xiaoming was playing someone who'd been in a terrible car accident.

ZHANG WEI. No need for that. You've got a spiteful tongue, you know that? No wonder I'm the only person you talk to.

ZHANG LIN. I speak to Ming Da Ma all the time.

ZHANG WEI. That nosy Party cat from next door! That's who you talk to?

ZHANG LIN. And my students.

ZHANG WEI. Standing on rooftops! Shouting into the wind, 'I am crazy! I succeed!', or chatting about TV shows with a dying old woman, is that a life?

ZHANG LIN. She's not dying.

ZHANG WEI. Is that / success?

ZHANG LIN. She's not dying, / why would you –

ZHANG WEI. Are you stupid? Can you hear that?

ZHANG LIN *turns off the TV. Listens to* MING XIAOLI *cough. Beat.*

ZHANG LIN. She has a chest infection.

ZHANG WEI. *You* have a chest infection, the infection is here – (*Points at his heart.*) Look at this place. You make good money, you can't buy some new curtains, a lamp? You could at least get a new TV, you spend enough time sitting in front of it, watching – what is this shit?

ZHANG LIN. I believe it's called *I Want To Become a Stewardess*.

ZHANG WEI. Turn it off.

ZHANG WEI *reaches for the remote,* ZHANG LIN *bats him away. Beat.*

If she was alive, she'd be so ashamed of you.

,

If you're not sleeping again, you should see a / doctor –

ZHANG LIN. I sleep fine.

,

ZHANG WEI. I'll phone you in the week. Don't ignore my call.

ZHANG LIN *drains his beer. Goes to the fridge to get another.*

Sure, have another beer.

ZHANG WEI *exits.* ZHANG LIN *turns the TV to the AV channel. The opening music and narration of* Casablanca. *Pause. Then he opens his laptop, plugs a microphone into it. Mutes the TV. Drains his beer. Hits a control on the laptop, picks up the microphone, speaks into it.*

ZHANG LIN. The 1st of May. 1989. It was hot. I think it was hot. I was eighteen years old. We were both eighteen years old.

We find ourselves in Tiananmen Square in 1989. YOUNG ZHANG LIN *is sitting on the floor, backpack next to him. He is very hot.* LIULI *enters, in a white dress.*

YOUNG ZHANG LIN. Are you okay?

LIULI. I'm fine. Fussing like an old woman.

He goes to kiss her. She covers her mouth.

My breath.

YOUNG ZHANG LIN. How can you throw up, you've barely eaten all week? Here. Have a peach.

YOUNG ZHANG LIN *takes out a bag of peaches.*

LIULI. We're supposed to be on hunger strike, you can't wait till we leave the square? If the cameras see you –

YOUNG ZHANG LIN. My mother always said it's important to eat fruit every day.

LIULI. Your mother called you Dog-face. Your whole family still call you Dog-face, you know why? Because you're still a little baby. A little boy –

Lights up on ZHANG LIN, *in front of the laptop, as he becomes aware of* MING XIAOLI *coughing through the wall.*

ZHANG LIN. A little boy. A little boy, a little –

1989 disappears as in 2012, the coughing grows louder, and ZHANG LIN *slams the laptop shut. Pause. He turns the TV up loud. Opens the fridge.* LIULI *is inside. She wears a red version of the white dress she wears in 1989, and shivers.* ZHANG LIN *closes the door.*

ACT TWO

Scene One

*Denver, Colorado. October 3rd, 2012. The night of the first
presidential debate. A dive bar. Some drunk Republicans. Some
drunk Democrats.* JOE *and* MEL *at the bar, nursing beers.*

MEL. No but I mean you really have to, you know, look at
  yourself, don't you, if you can't hold your own against a man
  named after a fucking *glove*.

JOE. It's just the first debate.

MEL. A fucking Mormon glove.

JOE. Listen, if we do this. If we find him –

MEL. Okay, Hildy Johnson, cool your boots. Look at you, take
  one meeting in a park, suddenly you think you're a reporter.

JOE. I am a reporter. And I'm excited by this, aren't you?

MEL. Sure.

JOE. So what's the first question you'd ask?

MEL. Okay, good, number one: what did he say to the soldier in
  the tank? Number two: what was in his shopping bags,
  number three: what does he eat for breakfast?

JOE. You'd ask the Unknown Hero whether he has toast or
  cereal?

MEL. See, this is what you don't understand about writing, it's
  the detail, it's the human interest, the small intimacies of
  great souls. You sure we can trust this guy, Zhang Lin?

JOE. Oh, for sure. He's pretty straight, serious, kind of sad, he
  lost his wife, before I knew him, they were like teenage
  sweethearts –

MEL. Okay don't look now but Michelle Bachmann is eating
  the biggest plate of ribs you ever –

JOE. *Hey.*

MEL. What? I'm listening.

JOE. So we start by combing Chinatown. Every shop, every bar, every nail salon.

MEL. Uh-uh. You got a strategy?

JOE. Well, I guess we just start off by asking people.

MEL. That's it?

JOE. Yeah. I mean, no. I had another idea.

MEL. Yeah? Is it as good as 'we ask people'?

JOE. Shut up, okay, we don't know shit, but what do we know? We know his name. And we know that he has a political conscience. So you check the electoral roll, you get his address, right?

MEL. No.

JOE. What d'you mean 'no', don't just / say 'no' like –

MEL. If he's in New York, he's probably illegal. He won't be registered to vote – Maria! Hey, over here!

MEL *has spotted* MARIA DUBIECKI, *a Democrat senator in her fifties, accompanied by* DAVID BARKER (*twenties*). MEL *waves to her.* MARIA *comes over, followed by* DAVID.

MARIA. Hi, boys. Little late for you to be out on a school night, isn't it?

MEL. Yeah, but I borrowed my dad's ID, what are you drinking?

MARIA. I'll have a spritzer, thank you, dear.

MEL. So, you been raiding Hillary Clinton's closet again?

MARIA. Oh I know, I know, it's awful, isn't it? It's just Wednesdays I always let my daughter pick my outfit, she's nine, she has terrible taste. Are they wasabi peas?

MEL. Knock yourself out, Senator.

MARIA *moves to the table, hungrily eats the wasabi peas.*

JOE. You look radiant, really.

MARIA. Well, thank you, Joe, I'm running on about four hours sleep a night these days, but I sleep in a Tupperware box, and eat nothing but steamed kale, so.

JOE. Well, it's working for you. (*To* DAVID.) Hi, I'm Joe, how you doing?

MARIA. Oh, where are my manners, this is my legislative assistant, Dave, this is Joe.

DAVID. David. David Barker. Hey.

> JOE *and* MEL *shake hands with* DAVID. *The* BARMAID *hands* MARIA *her spritzer.*

MEL. So listen, I hear Obama's lining you up for Education.

MARIA. Well, I don't know who could've given you that idea, it's almost like you plucked it from the blue sky to test my poker face, isn't it? How am I doing?

MEL. Oh my God, you could teach a Sphinx how to Sphinx.

JOE. So, Maria, how's morale in the spin room? I hear Barack's back on the Marlboros again…

MARIA. Shhh, don't tell Michelle –

DAVID. Senator, you have a conference call.

MARIA. No I don't, Dave. I need the bathroom. These Spanx are cutting me in half, would you hold this for me? Thanks, look at this place, you could get roofied just by breathing – nice seeing you, boys. Vote, vote, vote.

> MARIA *thrusts her drink at* DAVID *and goes. An awkward beat, then* DAVID *follows her.*

MEL. You seen her husband lately? Quit his job, full-time hausfrau, man looks like someone ran him over with a panzer.

JOE (*shrugs*). Don't have kids.

MEL. That's what I'm saying.

JOE. You have two.

MEL. That's what I'm saying. Don't have 'em.

JOE's cellphone rings. He checks it. MEL *gestures.*

Go ahead. You got a smoke?

JOE hands MEL *his rollie,* MEL *takes it, exits,* JOE *takes the call. Split scene, lights up on* FRANK, *he's getting a massage from a Chinese woman in his office. Cellphone in his hand.*

FRANK. You want to hear a story?

JOE. Ah, we're kind of in the middle of / something here –

FRANK. Trust me, you want to hear this story: four months ago, in June this year, a woman places a long-distance call to China from Manhattan. She places two adverts in the *Beijing Evening News*. One reads: 'In memory of the mothers who lost on 64'.

'

Joey? Are you listening?

JOE. 64, that's June 4th right? That's the massacre, that's Tiananmen?

FRANK. Correct. You want to know what the second ad said? The second ad said: 'To Wang Pengfei. The Unknown Hero of the square.'

JOE. The Unknown Hero, that's the Tank Man, and Wang Pengfei, that's – are you serious?

FRANK. The girl on the desk takes down the copy, the woman pays in yuan by credit card. And upstairs in his office, some middle-aged Chinese guy yells 'go to print'.

JOE. It was *published*? No. It would have been censored, right?

FRANK. The girl on the advertising desk is nineteen years old. She wasn't born when Tiananmen happened, most of her generation don't *know* it happened, it's been erased from the history books, so when some lady calls up with a bunch of coded messages about one of the worst fucking atrocities in her country's *history*, the girl doesn't think anything but 'how long till lunch?' That's the beauty of censorship.

JOE. So it just gets published? And the Party saw it?

FRANK. Sure the Party saw it. The editor gets fired. The girl gets fired, obviously, can't get a reference, doesn't even know what she's done wrong. Her family are paupers, think a cup of coffee is luxury goods, they cook their food over *dung*, Joe, over *dung*, you get the picture, this is not a girl for whom there is no place like home, so when a friend of a friend of a friend says 'I can get you to New York' /she –

JOE. She thinks she's on a one-way ticket to a Woody Allen movie.

FRANK. Right.

JOE. Except?

FRANK. Sure, except she's got no qualifications, basic English, no work permit and a bunch of fucking Triads breathing down her neck, she winds up in the Garment District, sleeping on the dressing-room floor of a fucking strip club.

,

JOE. Oh, right. So how did you meet her, Frank?

FRANK. None of your fucking business.

JOE. During your missionary work, I guess?

,

FRANK. Her name's Mary Chang. Get back to me when you've climbed off your high horse and I'll give you her number. She's expecting your call.

FRANK *hangs up.* JOE *looks around as* MEL *returns.*

MEL. What happened?

JOE. We got a lead.

Scene Two

A strip club in the Garment District. MARY CHANG *is dancing to a remix of 'China Girl'.*

We join her backstage having finished her dance, she wears a towelling robe over her costume. MEL *and* JOE *sit with her. A* GIRL *in the background, similarly dressed in robe and heels, oblivious of them, smoking a cigarette and reading the* National Enquirer.

MARY. They always make me dance to that same shit song.

MARY *takes out her earplugs.*

I only have like five minute. They don't like you have guest back here.

MEL. We only want a minute of your time, ma'am.

MARY (*to* MEL). You are friend of Frank too?

MEL. Friend is kind of a strong word.

MARY. I only met him one or two times, but he is so nice to me.

JOE. Yeah, he's a real do-gooder.

MARY. I google him. He works in a newspaper, right? You think he will give me a job?

JOE. Uh, I don't know.

MARY. Cos I use to work on newspaper in China, you know this?

JOE. Yeah, I'm sorry to hear about what happened with that.

MARY. Not my fault, you know? You know what they did to my people?

JOE. Yeah. It was pretty famous here.

MARY. They shot them! I don't know this!

MEL. Listen, Mary, we know it's kind of a long shot but – you don't remember the name of the woman who placed the advertisements, do you?

MARY. The woman who ruin my life? Yeah, I remember. Feng Meihui. I have my notebook still, you can check?

JOE. No, that's – Feng Meihui? You think that was her real name?

MARY (*shrugs*). Unless she had fake credit card. You look for her? Yeah? You find her – you tell her: 'thank you for nothing', right? 'Mary Chang say "fuck you".'

JOE takes two hundred dollars out of his wallet.

JOE. Here. That's for you.

Gives it to her. MARY *counts it. Looks up.*

MARY. You want me to dance?

JOE. No – no I don't, please, it's for your time. For your help.

A WOMAN looks in.

WOMAN. Mary. Ellie-May. Two minutes.

MARY glances at her, nods. The GIRL in the background tosses her magazine, takes off her robe. She's wearing a sequined stars-and-stripes bikini. She blasts some hairspray at her hair. MARY takes a piece of A4 paper folded five times from the gap between her shoe and her instep. She smoothes it out, gives it to JOE.

MARY. My résumé. You give to Frank? I don't know when he will come here again. I sent him email but he don't reply.

JOE. Sure. I'll make sure he gets that.

WOMAN (*off*). Mary! Move your ass!

MARY. I have to go. Some guy booked us for United Nations.

MARY takes off her robe and goes. JOE *looks at* MEL.

JOE. What does that even mean?

MEL. I'll tell you when you're older.

Scene Three

ZHANG LIN's apartment. ZHANG LIN sits. Laptop open. The microphone plugged in. A beer bottle, nearly empty, ZHANG LIN drains it. Looks at the refrigerator. Hesitates. Then picks up the microphone, hits a control on the laptop, begins recording. Lights down on ZHANG LIN as we find ourselves in 1989. YOUNG ZHANG LIN on the floor, as before, backpack next to him. LIULI enters, in her white dress.

LIULI. Tell me again about how we met.

YOUNG ZHANG LIN. No. It'll make me think about food.

LIULI. Why?

YOUNG ZHANG LIN. Because of the refrigerator!

LIULI. Tell me.

She pinches him. He cries out, whips his arm away.

Tell me.

'

YOUNG ZHANG LIN. My bed was broken. I was walking to buy a new bed. I had the money in my pocket. I'm walking down the street and I see this woman in the window of a store, a store that sells appliances. And she's electric. She's so beautiful, I have to stop for a moment and watch her, as she opens the door of this brand-new refrigerator and looks inside. And I cannot stop watching this. And I thought, whatever I have to do, whatever it takes, I've got to, I've got to have… that refrigerator.

LIULI shrieks, hits him in delighted outrage. YOUNG ZHANG LIN laughs, fends her off.

That refrigerator would change my life, so I go in and I hand over the money in my pocket. And the store owner helps me carry it home. And I plug in my refrigerator and it starts to hum. And I already feel like a different person.

I fall asleep and when I wake up it's hot in my apartment so I think, I know, I'll put my face into the cold refrigerator. So I open the door and this girl jumps out. The girl from the store, she's hidden inside my beautiful new machine. A stowaway. She's been there the whole time.

Like a rat on a ship. Like a spider in a crate of melons.

She's shivering. Her eyelashes are frosted up. She says 'I'm so cold.' I touch her skin and she is, she's freezing. I think, she's going to die if I don't do something, so I say, let's go to bed. It's warmer there. She nods and her teeth clatter together like spoons in a bowl. So I take her hand. Her cold little hand.

And then I remembered, I don't have a bed. I spent my money on a refrigerator. I completely forgot, I was supposed to buy a bed.

So we made love on the floor instead.

He looks at her. A kiss. In 2012, a knock on the door.
ZHANG LIN *switches off the microphone. 1989 disappears.*
ZHANG WEI *enters, wearing a face mask, a cardboard box under his arm.*

ZHANG WEI (*Mandarin*). You alright?

ZHANG LIN (*Mandarin*). Yeah. You?

ZHANG WEI. I bought you some new dishes. They're seconds. From work. The glaze is flawed, but you can eat off them fine.

ZHANG LIN. I don't need new dishes.

ZHANG WEI. Yours are all chipped. It harbours bacteria, it's unhygienic.

ZHANG LIN. You shouldn't go out, not when the smog's like this.

ZHANG WEI. You can just say 'thank you', you know that? You can just say 'thank you, Zhang Wei, for thoughtfully buying me new dishes'.

ZHANG LIN. It's from the factories, you know?

ZHANG WEI. Sure. The factories and the trucks. They're talking about suspending production. Stressing me out, we're behind schedule as it is. By the way, have you spoken to Joe yet?

ZHANG LIN. Yeah. Yeah. Yeah. Yeah.

ZHANG WEI *puts down the box, turns to leave.*

Zhang Wei? Zhang Wei?

ZHANG WEI. What?

ZHANG LIN. Thank you for the dishes.

ZHANG WEI. You're welcome.

ZHANG LIN. Will you get me a beer?

ZHANG WEI *goes.* ZHANG LIN *looks at the refrigerator. Hesitates. Opens the door.* LIULI *is inside. She hands him a beer. He takes it, closes the door. Yanks the plug from the socket.*

Scene Four

JOE's *dingy apartment.* TESS, *taking it in, as* JOE *produces a number of large folders, lays them on the floor.*

JOE. And you found it okay?

TESS. Your streets are too long.

JOE. Well, you'll have to take that up with the Dutch. You want a beer?

TESS. I can't stay.

JOE. No, sure, I just wanted to – I felt kind of awful, about how I spoke to you the other night, and – anyway so I sorted through my China archive. They might not be of any interest to you, they're mostly still-life or landscape but… for the credit card, I mean?

TESS. Oh. Thank you. That's – wow, thanks.

TESS *opens a folder.* JOE *realises his mistake. A panic.*

JOE. No, sorry, that's not. That's the wrong, you don't want to look at those –

But TESS *has taken a printout and is examining it.*

Tess, please. Don't. I didn't mean to –

He goes to take it from her, she moves it out of his reach, still looking at it. JOE *hesitates.*

Sudan. '94, I think.

TESS *goes to the next print.*

That's Colombia.

Pause. He points to a detail on the print.

He was a trade unionist. Worked at a Coca-Cola bottling plant in Carepa.

Pause. The next print. JOE *points to a detail on it.*

That's the paramilitaries arriving.

Pause. The next print. TESS *covers her mouth.* JOE *indicates something.*

The light wasn't good. I followed them into the bushes but I couldn't risk a flash.

TESS *puts down the print. A pause. Then she takes a breath. And picks up another.*

That's a cemetery in Gaza. Palestinian woman, that's her boys in the background.

TESS. You must have been standing, quite close…

JOE. Pretty close yeah.

,

TESS. You can see every wrinkle / in her –

JOE. You see the flare coming off that iron bar in her hand, I love that, total fluke.

TESS. Looks like she's about to –

JOE. Yeah. Caught me right across the eye. See?

He shows TESS *his scar. She feels it.*

The restaurant. I'm sorry about, you know –

TESS. Throwing a wobbly?

JOE. Yeah. I guess.

TESS. S'alright. I had a toffee apple.

She retracts her hand.

Can I see the Tank Man?

JOE *finds a print of the Tank Man photograph in a folder. Gives it to her. She examines it.*

Have you found him yet?

JOE *shakes his head. She looks at the print.*

I always used to wonder about his shopping bags.

JOE. Why is everyone so hung up on that, what he bought from the *store* that morning?

TESS. Because I think that's amazing. A man goes out to buy a paper, or a new shirt or something, and by the end of the day, he's part of history.

JOE *takes out his tobacco, rolls a cigarette.*

JOE. Yeah but, forget the shopping, that's not – that's a picture of heroism, it really, it changed things, you know?

TESS. Yeah but don't most of your photos do that?

JOE. Fuck no. I wish.

'

What?

TESS. No, I just. I can't work out if you're Piglet or Eeyore.

JOE *fumbles his tobacco.* TESS *takes the papers from him, she rolls the cigarette, deftly.*

So why d'you bother then? If you think taking pictures can't change anything –

JOE. Because it used to.

TESS. The Vietnam War wasn't lost on the battlefields of Vietnam, it was lost in the living rooms of America, right?

JOE. Right! Right, and that *was* because of photographs. No one could forget what was happening out there when the blood was right there in technicolour for the very first time.

But living rooms now, they're full of war. Full of famine, full of genocide. Atrocity's just another pattern in the chintz.

,

TESS. I bet you're really fun at parties, aren't you?

JOE. Look, I'm not saying – I don't think there's more tragedy in the world, I just think, well I guess there are just more cameras. There are schoolkids armed with iPhones who do my job way better than me now. And it seems like, well to me anyway, it seems like maybe photographs are like people. The more there are of them, the less any individual one means.

But, you know, I don't know how to do anything else. Kodak ergo sum. I read that somewhere, I didn't come up with that or anything, you want a beer?

TESS. No, I. I have to go in a minute.

JOE. Come on. I'm trying to apologise here.

TESS. By talking about Vietnam?

JOE. I said I was trying, I didn't say I was good at it. Come on, have a beer with me. Or tea, I have tea, you guys like that, right?

,

TESS. I prefer beer.

JOE *grins, gets two beers, opens them.*

So why don't you want kids?

JOE. World's a shitty place. Seems kind of unfair to bring a child into that. And, you know, I just get really violent when I'm drunk, so. Cheers.

He hands her a beer. Clinks her bottle with his. They drink. He opens a correct folder of prints for her. She looks through them, picks one up.

TESS. Oh, wow. This is it, that's just, can I have this?

JOE. That? I just took that one to test a new lens. Don't you think it's kind of / bland?

TESS. Bland, yes, it's perfect. I love it. It's so… white-bread.

JOE. Then have it. You probably want a high-res TIFF, right?

TESS *nods.* JOE *opens his laptop, keeps working, finding and sending the file,* TESS *hands him the rollie, he lights it, smokes. She looks at his tobacco packet. She takes out her straights.*

TESS. *American Spirit.* Will you throw me out if I smoke an immoral Marlboro?

JOE. Sure, go on. You can say your Hail Marys after.

TESS *laughs. Lights a cigarette. Pause.*

TESS. I was really glad you called. I don't really know anyone in New York. Except this drug dealer I bought some speed off when I first got here.

JOE. I used to take so much speed in the nineties. I stayed up for four days once, in Kosovo.

TESS. She keeps calling me up crying all the time, wants to talk about her boyfriend. She came round last night with a *Sex and the City* box-set. She made me plait her hair. She keeps making me say 'oregano', then laughing. If I still lived in London, she's exactly the kind of woman I would avoid at all costs. She's my only friend in New York.

JOE *keeps his eyes on the screen.*

JOE. Nah, you got at least two.

Outside, it starts to rain. TESS *looks out of the window, drinks her beer. Smokes.*

TESS. They can control the weather, you know.

JOE. What?

TESS. In Beijing. They fire rockets, into the sky, to disperse the clouds.

If they don't want it to rain, then it doesn't. Terrifying.

She looks around; at JOE, *and at his gloomy apartment.*

I'm going to buy you a lamp.

Scene Five

JOE *consults* MICHELLE, *an Asian-American NYPD cop for information.* MICHELLE *is in the middle of an arrest with her partner,* OFFICER HYTE, *outside a house in Harlem. Blue flashing lights from off.* MICHELLE *is wearing disposable gloves and tagging an enormous bag of white powder.*

MICHELLE. This is a one-off, okay? Why you so interested in Chinese newspapers?

JOE. C'mon, Shelly, I'm a voracious reader, you know that.

MICHELLE. Okay. So we have three Feng Meihuis on record in Manhattan. One, she died last year, the second's in Penn State, attacked a real-estate agent with a fire iron. The last one lives in Chinatown, on Mott Street. Clean record except for a speeding ticket up in Maine in 2002, one daughter. It's a fish stall –

JOE. Address?

MICHELLE (*chiding*). *Please.* I wrote it down for you. If I get a report in of some sweet Chinese businesswoman being harassed by some prick with a camera I will find you and throw away the key.

JOE. Remind me why we broke up?

OFFICER HYTE *leads out a* DEALER *clad in garish Bermuda shorts.*

MICHELLE. Because you were cheating on me with the Lebanon.

DEALER....I know my rights!

MICHELLE. Great, well, Officer Hyte's gonna remind you of them anyway.

* OFFICER HYTE. You have the right to remain silent, anything you say may later be used against you in court, you have the right to consult with an attorney and have attorney present with you during questioning, if you cannot afford an attorney, you have the right to an attorney appointed at public expense.

* JOE (*grins*). How're the kids?

MICHELLE. Hannah's got head lice and Liam hit a Little Leaguer in the face with a sports sock full of pennies.

JOE. Ouch. What'd you do?

MICHELLE. Put him in a cell for a half hour with a really mean hooker.

JOE. Nice job.

MICHELLE. Protect and serve.

MICHELLE *and* OFFICER HYTE *lead the* DEALER *away.*

Scene Six

The back of a Chinatown fish stall. MEL *checks his phone as* JOE *takes shots on his camera. His natural instinct.* JENNIFER LEE *enters, dragging her mother,* FENG MEIHUI. *Both in aprons, pink with fish-blood.* MEIHUI *sees* JOE, *alarmed.*

MEIHUI. No photo. No photo.

JOE. Sorry. Feng Meihui?

He shakes her hand.

MEIHUI. This, my daughter. Jennifer.

JOE. Hi. Joe Schofield. This is Mel Stanwyck, he's a writer.

MEL. Thanks for speaking with us.

MEIHUI (*nods*). You got the money?

MEL. Yeah.

MEIHUI. You give it?

JOE *looks at* MEL. MEL *nods.* JOE *hands the money to* MEIHUI.

I do this for her. She going to college in the fall. We need money.

MEL. Absolutely, ma'am. So, we wanted to speak with you about a couple of advertisements you placed in the *Beijing*

Evening News earlier this year. The first one. Mothers of 64. 64 means June 4th? Tiananmen Square, right? I'm sorry to ask but did you lose someone?

MEIHUI *looks at* JENNIFER. *Nods her permission.*

JENNIFER. My brother. We were twins.

MEIHUI. They were very small, babies. We were in the apartment. Bullet, comes through the window. Into the kitchen. Into the crib.

JOE. I'm so sorry.

MEIHUI (*to* JENNIFER). I need a Fresca. Get me a Fresca.

JENNIFER *goes out.* MEIHUI *takes out a picture, shows* JOE *and* MEL.

This is him. On the left. When I have twins, I think, 'I am so lucky' right? I beat the one-child policy. They get you in the end.

MEL. The second advertisement. About the Unknown Hero –

MEIHUI. I don't know nothing about that.

MEL. You placed it though, right?

MEIHUI. I do it for someone else. He don't have a credit card.

MEL. Could you tell us his name?

MEIHUI *shakes her head.* JENNIFER *comes back with the Fresca.* MEIHUI *takes it, cracks it open, slurps. Scratches her leg.* JOE *takes out more money, gives it to her. Pause.*

MEIHUI. He call himself Jimmy Wang. You don't hassle him, right?

MEL. Is it possible his Chinese name might be Pengfei? Wang Pengfei?

MEIHUI. Possible. I don't know.

JOE. The advertisement. You placed it for Jimmy as a favour. Like, guanxi?

MEIHUI (*laughs*). Not guanxi. Just money. People pay me, I do them a favour. They don't pay me –

MEL. You don't, right, so how do you know him?

MEIHUI *shrugs*. MEL *nods,* JOE *gives her more money. They wait.* MEIHUI, *uneasy.*

I promise you, ma'am, this won't go any further –

MEIHUI. I help him come. Into the country.

MEL. Thank you, and when was this?

MEIHUI (*thinks*). Fall. Maybe October 1989.

JOE. 1989. You're sure?

MEIHUI. Yeah because he was one of the first we help, after we come here. He stay in safe house near New York State border. We wait till river freeze. Drive them over.

MEL. Okay. And where is he now?

MEIHUI (*shrugs*). I put them always at Brooklyn Bridge. He worked in restaurant. Then some flower store for a time but… now I don't know. I don't see him for months.

MEL. Which flower store?

MEIHUI. I don't know! My friend Fan, she work in funeral home, over in Flushing. He used to bring them white uh, *ju hua*?

She speaks to JENNIFER *in Mandarin: 'What's the word?'*

JENNIFER. Chrysanthemums.

JOE *shows her the picture of the Tank Man.*

JOE. Do you know who this man is?

MEHUI. Yeah, I know. He's famous. He's a famous man.

JENNIFER *takes the picture. Scrutinises it.*

JOE. Did you bring him to New York?

MEIHUI *says nothing.* MEL *nods at* JOE. JOE *gives her more money. She puts it in her pocket.*

Did you bring him to New York?

MEIHUI. No.

JOE (*pissed off*). How do we know you're telling the truth?

MEIHUI. Why should I lie? You think I talk with people like you for fun?

JOE. Maybe you could ask your boss / if he –

MEIHUI. Boss?

JOE. Like, I don't know, boss like – *Godfather*? You know that movie?

MEIHUI. No Godfather. Just me. American dream. Family business. My sister in Fuzhou make documents, her husband is Passport Inspector, very good, I deliver client to the safe house, collect the money. Family business. I help China. Money goes back there. You know how much poor there are there still? Not us –

MEIHUI*'s pride erodes her bad temper, she looks at* JENNIFER, *loving*.

She gonna be next Hillary Clinton!

JOE. You like Hillary huh?

MEIHUI. Last election, I give a thousand dollars to Hillary Clinton.

JOE. You did? How come?

MEIHUI. She helps illegals get papers. To be associated with such great a figure. Is an honour. Women hold up half the sky, right?

You go now?

JOE. Yeah. Thank you.

MEIHUI *goes out.* MEL *follows her out to the front of the store.*

MEL. You coming?

JOE *nods, as* MEIHUI *comes back holding something in her gloved hands.*

MEIHUI. Here. You want a fish?

JOE. Uh, sure. What is it?

MEIHUI. Pollock. Like cod. Very good.

> MEIHUI *speaks to* JENNIFER *in Mandarin, telling her to wrap the fish.*

JOE. Well, thanks.

> MEIHUI *goes.* JENNIFER *does as she's told. Gives* JOE *the wrapped fish.*

JENNIFER. If you find him, tell him 'Li Jiang's sister says, "have a nice day".'

Scene Seven

JOE *and* MEL. *The Glorious City Flower Shop, Queens. Buckets of flowers, a cash register. Amid various Interflora posters, a yellowing campaign poster from 2008 for Hillary Clinton.*

MEL. I need a drink. Ninety flower stores in three days. Sinuses are fucking on fire.

JOE. I told you, take a pill or something. This is the last one on the / list, just –

> MEL *sneezes.* PENGSI *enters.*

MEL. Hi, my name is Mel Stanwyck, this is Joe Schofield, lovely store you have here, I don't know if you can help us out, we're looking for someone called Jimmy Wang? Or Wang Pengfei? We're not cops.

PENGSI. Sorry, not here.

MEL. No one of that name working here?

PENGSI. No. I can't help you.

MEL. There are apartments upstairs, right? I saw the air-con units.

PENGSI. No, he doesn't live there.

MEL. Okay, well, thanks for your time.

MEL *makes to leave,* JOE *holds his position.*

JOE. So where *does* he live then?

PENGSI. What?

MEL. What are you doing?

JOE. He didn't answer the question, he just said he doesn't live *upstairs* so – (*To* PENGSI.) so where *does* he live?

PENGSI. I don't… sorry, I don't understand?

MEL. Joe, he doesn't know / anything –

JOE. Wait a second – do you know this man? We're not cops.

MEL. Will you leave the guy in peace? Let's go. I need a piss.

JOE. Just give me a second, alright! Sorry, I promise you, I'm not a cop, just, take a look at the picture.

PENGSI *scrutinises the picture. Shakes his head, hands the photo back.* PENGSI'S WIFE *enters.*

He doesn't live there, that's what you said, not you don't know him, 'he doesn't live there', so, so –

MEL. Joe, that's enough.

JOE. So I'm just wondering what you meant by that?

PENGSI. I didn't mean nothing. My English is… not good. I'm sorry.

PENGSI *and his* WIFE *speak in Mandarin as* MEL *addresses* JOE.

* PENGSI'S WIFE. Who are they?

PENGSI. Just cops, go upstairs.

* MEL (*sneezes*). This is not how you do this, you can't walk into a guy's store and Columbo him just cos English isn't his first language!

PENGSI *turns back to* JOE.

PENGSI. Can I help you with anything else?

MEL *looks at* JOE.

MEL. I'm catching a cab.

MEL *exits*. JOE *hesitates*.

PENGSI'S WIFE (*English*). You want to buy something?

,

JOE. Yeah. Sorry, yeah I, can I get some flowers?

PENGSI'S WIFE *exits*.

PENGSI. Sure. Uh. What do you want?

JOE. Uh – roses? Roses are nice, right?

As PENGSI *starts to gather and wrap a bunch of yellow roses,* JOE *takes out his phone, surreptitiously takes a shot of* PENGSI. *His thumbs move as he quickly types an email. He sends it. Lights up on* ZHANG LIN, *slumped at his table as his iPhone beeps. He picks it up, reads the email. Quickly deletes it, consumed with rage. He calls* JOE. *Split scene between* JOE *and* ZHANG LIN.

Hey, Zhang Lin!

ZHANG LIN. What is wrong with you?

JOE. What the –

ZHANG LIN. Do you think you are double-oh-seven James Bond? You don't put such fucking words in an email to me, okay?

JOE. What? What words?

ZHANG LIN. You think an email like that from an American journalist does not get seen by the censors? 'Tank man', in the subject line, Joe, in the subject line, are you stupid or something?

,

JOE (*appalled*). Shit. Shit, what a fucking moron, I didn't think, I'm so sorry, I was, I got carried away – what I can do, can we fix this or –

ZHANG LIN. Fuck you.

JOE. You sound a little – it must be three in the morning there, what are you –

ZHANG LIN. I'm not sleeping very... good, well. I'm not sleeping well. My neighbour, Ming Xiaoli, she's dying.

JOE. What's the matter with her?

ZHANG LIN. She has Beijing Lung, I think. She coughs through the wall all night, I can't sleep with it. Why haven't you called Benny?

JOE. Who?

ZHANG LIN. My nephew, you promised my brother you would –

JOE. Sure, I'll call him tomorrow, but what about the email, can I do anything there?

,

ZHANG LIN. Just call Benny.

ZHANG LIN hangs up. JOE looks at his phone. Lights down on ZHANG LIN. PENGSI hands JOE the flowers.

PENGSI. Fifteen dollars.

JOE. Uh. Thanks. That's – shit, I'm sorry, I'm a little light on cash.

PENGSI. It's no problem. We take American Express. Or Visa.

Lights down on JOE and PENGSI, we rejoin ZHANG LIN in his apartment.

Scene Eight

ZHANG LIN *sits, turns on the TV, play a movie. Perhaps the first few lines or opening bars of the score to* Casablanca. *Then* ZHANG LIN *mutes the TV, opens his laptop, his face is lit by the screen. The microphone is plugged in, he hits the controls.*

ZHANG LIN. When I look back, it seems obvious, and I feel stupid. But I want to be honest. And I was stupid. If I wasn't, I would've put her in a taxi. I would have carried her home on my back. I would've told the English journalist to go away. In my head, I've done all of these things.

We see YOUNG ZHANG LIN *and* LIULI *in 1989.*

YOUNG ZHANG LIN. You need to eat something.

LIULI. It's too acidic.

YOUNG ZHANG LIN. No, okay, but – Liuli.

LIULI. It's my body.

YOUNG ZHANG LIN. So I don't have a say?

LIULI. You have a say. You just can't make me.

YOUNG ZHANG LIN. You're going to have a baby, you have to eat –

LIULI. Why?

YOUNG ZHANG LIN. Because, because I'm your husband and I'm ordering you to.

LIULI grabs the bag of peaches, takes one and eats it, hungrily. Juice running down her face. She wipes her hand across her chin. YOUNG ZHANG LIN *laughs.*

You pig. You piglet. Come here.

LIULI shakes her head. Defiant.

Come here.

She relents, jumps into his arms, wrapping her legs around him. They kiss.

LIULI. We're going to have a baby.

YOUNG ZHANG LIN. Don't draw attention. We don't have a licence.

KATE, *a British reporter in a flak jacket, enters, followed by a* CAMERAMAN.

KATE. Excuse me? Do you speak English?

YOUNG ZHANG LIN. I do. My wife doesn't.

LIULI. What does she want? Is she a journalist?

KATE. I wonder if I might talk to you?

LIULI. Let me speak to her –

YOUNG ZHANG LIN. Shh, she won't understand you.

LIULI *looks at* KATE, *laughs. Somewhere, speakers blast Beethoven's 'Ode to Joy'. Tinny and distorted.* KATE *gestures to her* CAMERAMAN *to record* LIULI. *During this, coughing starts, off.*

LIULI. We're going to have a baby. It's going to be born in the future. It's going to be a great artist. It's going to be a doctor. It's going to own a shop. It's going to have a doorbell with an electric chime. It's going to have a car with a refrigerator in it and a rubber dinghy and three pairs of Levi's. It's going to have five brothers and sisters who look just like it and all my children, will be fat and happy and clever and kind. You wait. Just you wait.

,

KATE. Can we check that / for sound?

ZHANG LIN. 'Can we check that for sound?' she said. I can find no record of this footage ever being televised.

MING XIAOLI *enters. She carries a large pot plant. Beat.*

MING XIAOLI. I brought you a plant. You have to water it once a week.

ZHANG LIN. Thank you.

MING XIAOLI. I want a striptease.

ZHANG LIN. I'm too tired.

MING XIAOLI (*tuts*). At my funeral.

ZHANG LIN. We don't need to talk about this now.

MING XIAOLI. They had one at my brother's, in Jiangsu, it was good fun. Cheered everyone up. And it helps to attract a crowd. I want a lot of / people –

ZHANG LIN. Ming Da Ma, don't –

MING XIAOLI. A lot of people having a good time, that's what I want. You'll have to call my daughter. I had a dream last night, she lectured me about smoking. She hit me with a coat hanger. This was in my own bedroom, only when I looked out of the window, we were by the sea and the sea was full of pigs.

ZHANG LIN. It was only a bad dream.

MING XIAOLI (*defensive*). I don't smoke.

MING XIAOLI *starts to cry.*

It's not fair. Telling me off, I never smoked in my whole life. She must've mixed me up with my sister. I'm a good girl. I was on a poster, you know. A Party poster, it was called 'Through Cooperation the Electric Light was Fixed'. I was twelve, I had to stand like this:

She stands, holds up her arm like the Statue of Liberty.

Holding out the light bulb. I stood like this for hours.

The effort it takes to keep her arm up is clear, but she continues, wheezing.

For months, everywhere I went, people had this picture of me on their walls.

ZHANG LIN. You'd think something like that would go to your head.

MING XIAOLI. Yes, it's amazing I stayed so modest.

ZHANG LIN *gently lowers her arm. She leans against him, regaining her breath.*

I hear you talking to your wife.

ZHANG LIN *doesn't respond. He picks up* MING XIAOLI*'s hands, massages them again.*

I don't mind. I remember you moving in. Seventeen years old. Children. I used to lie awake and listen to you making love. It made me happy. My husband was no great shakes in that department.

MING XIAOLI *breaks off, wracked with coughing.* ZHANG LIN *lets go of her hands. She covers her mouth with her sleeve. When she brings it down, there is a little blood on it.*

Gimme a beer.

ZHANG LIN. It's warm.

MING XIAOLI. So is the ground. Let's get drunk.

ACT THREE

Scene One

JOE*'s apartment. The yellow roses stuck in a jug. A new lamp.*
TESS *is bringing in stacks of files.* JOE *holds up the fish* FENG
MEIHUI *gave him and a bag of Doritos.*

JOE (*Dick Van Dyke*). 'Fish and chips.'

TESS (*laughs*). Idiot.

JOE. You just fry it with a little butter and lemon. Good for the
brain cells.

TESS. I don't cook. (*The flowers.*) Nice. Whose grave you nick
'em off?

JOE. No, they're for you.

TESS. Oh. Thanks, Joe. Listen, if you need to get off, I can /
just –

JOE. No, we have time, Mel's late, okay, these are the keys, the
heat's on a timer, I left you a fresh towel on the bed, in case
you want to, you know, like –

TESS. Wash?

JOE. Yeah.

TESS. It's all mod-cons here, isn't it?

JOE. I don't know what that means, by the way, I've got a pull-
out so you're welcome to stay on after I get back if you need
to –

TESS. I should be okay. Apparently they just need a day to fill
the apartment with chemicals, and then another day to sweep
up the corpses.

JOE. Okay. Only you brought a lot of stuff, I didn't know if /
you were –

TESS. I know, it's just, it's work. They brought my presentation forward, I'm totally fucked.

She takes a bottle of whiskey from her bag.

JOE. Uh-uh. (Very nice.) So quit.

JOE *fetches glasses. She pours them both a drink.*

TESS (*laughs*). Yeah, okay! And do what?

JOE. What? I don't know, go join the Red Cross or something, if you need the / super, his cell is –

TESS. Join the Red Cross?

JOE. I wasn't serious, I was just –

TESS. So why did you say it?

JOE. I was joking, it was a / joke –

TESS. No, I'm just interested in why would you / say something like –

JOE. I don't know! Cos I think you *would* be good at it, I guess, and you might get off on, doing something that has, you know, whatever more of… an effect.

TESS. I have an effect.

JOE. I wasn't, come on, you know what I mean.

TESS. No, Joe, what do you mean? Maybe I could set up a soup kitchen? Rescue some prostitutes? Go and work in a, in a children's home? Wear a nylon tabard, drug dealers trying to get in through the windows, rats and chicken dippers?

JOE. What the fuck's a tabard? I'm not suggesting you go dig wells in Africa, I / just –

TESS. Good. Cos I don't give a shit about Africa.

JOE. That's nice, Tess, very nice, d'you ever actually listen to the words that come out your mouth?

TESS. I don't know, do you ever step outside your pious, holier-than-thou, sanctimonious pedestal?

JOE. You can't step outside a pedestal. Just, forget I opened my mouth, gimme some of that.

He takes the whiskey, drinks. Passes it back. They pass the bottle between them in silence.

That's good whiskey.

The buzzer goes. JOE *answers it, opens the door.*

TESS. Yeah. Listen, Joe? I do give a shit about Africa.

JOE. I know.

MEL enters, in a flak jacket. He carries a backpack.

JOE. What are you wearing?

MEL. Statement of intent. Long Island on debate night. Place is going to be lousy with cooze, you got a new lamp.

JOE. Yeah. You like it?

MEL....no, is that whiskey?

MEL picks up the whiskey, pours himself a mug.

TESS. Hello, Mel.

MEL throws her a cursory glance.

MEL. Oh, hey, Tess, how you doing?

TESS. Great thanks. You?

MEL. Uh-uh. (*To* JOE.) We gotta go.

TESS turns. MEL *gestures to* JOE: *'Are you two...?',* JOE *shakes his head, mouths: 'No, shut up.'* MEL *puts his hands together, silently thanks the heavens.* JOE *double-checks his bag, goes out. An awkward pause between* TESS *and* MEL.

TESS. So. Second debate, right? Any predictions?

MEL. Romney's going to be ramping on China, no prizes for guessing that.

TESS. Sure, 'What if the big boy comes and steals our sweets?' Maybe they don't want your sweets.

MEL. Well, that's a radical interpretation of the facts. You know how much they've expanded their military? How much of Africa they've got in their shopping carts? Plus, you know, they seem pretty intent on putting every factory in Ohio out of business, so –

TESS. Yeah you lot've got a real bee in your bonnet about that, haven't you?

MEL. About thousands of American jobs going overseas? Yeah people get a little worked up! I don't know if you can imagine what losing your entire manufacturing industry to / another nation would –

TESS. Can I imagine? Oh, love, stable door, horse. We don't manufacture shit. Everything in Britain's been made in Taiwan since the sixties. Every child born since Thatcher has it stamped on its bottom. You want to see?

JOE enters, with his toothbrush, packs it.

MEL (*to* JOE). What is she even doing here?

JOE. Her apartment's / full of roaches!

TESS. You think you're a *liberal* because you're voting for the black guy? Obama can't even get a basic Medicare bill through intact, there's a good chance another Democrat term right now is the worst thing could happen to them, you let the Republicans break their neck on the fiscal cliff then, in 2016, if I had a vote, I'd vote for Hillary Clinton. And if I didn't have a vote I'd give her all the money in my pocket.

JOE (*sotto*). Oh / my God. Oh, shit.

He is suddenly feverish with excitement. JOE unzips his bag, takes his own out, starts it up, types.

MEL. If you don't like this country, I can get you a cab to JFK right now.

TESS (*to* JOE). What's up with you?

JOE. How do you change things if you don't have a vote? Money. No one poor ever got near the White House. Look – under federal law, all party contributions over $200 must be itemised, with the donor's occupation and employer.

MEL. So?

JOE. Remember what I said, in Denver? About checking the electoral roll, you laughed but maybe – look, you can search online.

   JOE *clicks on a link, Opensecrets.org.*

MEL (*points*). There –

JOE (*types*). No, I think we need to go back to '08. You pick your candidate –

MEL. Clinton? Think you're looking for a Hillary fan?

JOE. Just a hunch. Come on. Come on…

   JOE *scans the website. Clicks the next one. Scans. The next. Scans.*

MEL. There.

JOE. *Yes.* Jimmy Wang. Three hundred dollars.

MEL. Jimmy Wang, there must be a few of them, we don't know that's him.

JOE. But if it is, he was alive and solvent on the 14th of October, 2008. And if he's registered here that means there's a record of his address.

MEL. Yeah but we can't access that.

JOE. You know who could though, right?

   ,

MEL. She wouldn't. I mean, she wouldn't, that's got to be illegal, right?

JOE. She'll be down there in Long Island, right?

MEL. She's a Senator, Joe, she's a public servant, it's not cool.

JOE. But –

MEL. Not cool, Joe! Come on, I'm parked in front of a fire hydrant.

   MEL *grabs his bag, exits.* JOE *closes his laptop, puts it in his bag.*

TESS. Bye, Mel! Have a safe trip!

MEL (*bad English accent*). Tally-ho!

> JOE *picks up his bag. Hesitates. Gives* TESS *a hug. She is slightly surprised by this.*

JOE. Eat the fish. It's good.

> JOE *goes.* TESS *looks at the fish. Unwraps it. Picks up her phone. Dials.*

TESS. Hi, will you deliver to Hudson Heights? Okay, this is what I want:

Scene Two

FRANK *at a chess table in Washington Square Gardens, with a coffee.* JOE *enters.*

FRANK. You're late.

JOE. We said ten thirty. It's ten thirty.

FRANK. Well, I was early. You should've known I'd be early. You see what they did to this place? Fucking Giuliani. I slept in this square for a month when I was twenty-two. Over there. Amazing, isn't it, what a young body will tolerate. Tina made me go camping last summer, one night in a tent, I've been in physio four months.

JOE. Wait – you were homeless?

FRANK. God, no. Vietnam. There were about five hundred of us here. The stink of people, that's what I remember. I wore the same pair of jeans for a month straight.

JOE. You *protested*?

FRANK. That is not the big surprise. The big surprise is, I used to wear jeans.

> MEL *enters, bleary-eyed, hungover, muffled up against the cold.*

JOE. What's going on, Frank?

FRANK. Mel! You look like shit! How was Long Island?

MEL. Don't drink the iced tea.

JOE. Frank?

FRANK. I need you to drop the story.

,

JOE. Which story?

FRANK. The China story.

JOE. The Tank Man?

MEL. What?

JOE. Frank, come on, you can't – we haven't even found him yet.

FRANK. So you won't mind.

JOE. I do mind. I absolutely mind –

JOE *stands up*.

FRANK. I talked with Lou about it, she's not happy, / sit down.

JOE. Fuck Lou.

MEL. Woman's a bureaucrat.

JOE. She doesn't know the first thing about how a newspaper works –

FRANK. No. But she happens to be extremely talented at running the company that owns us. And Verico is seeking to acquire one cable network and two newspapers in the Asian territories. Which means it's seeking investment capital, and it's seeking it from about the only place in the world there is any right now.

,

JOE. China.

MEL. Ah, Jesus. Okay. Jesus.

FRANK. Am I saying I like it? No, but – and I'm sorry if this complicates your video-game view of the world – but Verico are not the bad guys. They're *trying* to keep thousands of employees from the breadline.

MEL. And China has them by the pocketbook.

FRANK. No, Mel, they have the whole country by the pocketbook. This is a means to an end.

JOE. It's collusion.

FRANK. I don't think it's possible to sum up what this is in just one word. Sit down.

JOE. You could fight this if you wanted.

FRANK. No, I couldn't, not in the way you want, sit down, Joe.

JOE. Why not?

FRANK. Because you get a lot of medical bills when your kid has leukaemia, it's kind of a side effect. Siddown.

'

MEL. Sit down, Joe.

JOE *sits*.

JOE. Okay, listen to me – you run a *newspaper*. You cover the *news*.

FRANK. Yeah well when you owe a guy one-point-three trillion dollars it's prudent not to make a big deal out the fact he knocks his wife around a little.

JOE. Anyway, you think the PSB read your newspaper?

FRANK. A month ago, Xi Jinping cancelled his meeting with Hillary Clinton because she criticised China's support for Assad. The *Times* has been blacked out for their investigation into the Chinese Prime Minister –

JOE. So? The Party's corrupt, everyone knows that, even a state-run media is covering *that* story, you really want to run a newspaper with less transparency than *The People's Daily*? You're supposed to be a guardian of a free fucking press –

FRANK. Do you think this is *vanity* publishing, what I get up at five a.m. every day to do? This newspaper is some sort of

catalogue of my favourite things, do I look like fucking
Oprah? Don't you dare sit there and suffer at me, hell I
suffer too! You think I enjoy using the word 'multi-
platform'? That I think it's *desirable* to employ the best
writers in the country, then stick a comments section under
their articles, so whatever no-neck grain-fucker from
Arkansas can chip in his five uninformed, mispelled, hateful
cents because God *forbid* an opinion should go unvoiced?
Assholes Anonymous validating each other in packs under
my banner, that's not a democratic press, it's a nationwide
circle-jerk for imbeciles.

JOE. Yeah, well the internet isn't going anywhere, so –

FRANK. I'm still hoping it's a fad. I have a meeting. Consider
yourself spiked.

JOE *advances on* FRANK.

Go on. You can hit me. If it makes you feel better.

JOE *knocks the coffee out of* FRANK*'s hand. It's a dismal
gesture and he knows it.* FRANK *takes out a handkerchief,
wipes the splashes from his shoes, pulls his coat round him.*

Fucking liberals. Too much spilt coffee, not enough split lips.

FRANK *leaves.* JOE *hollers after him.*

JOE. You voted for Bill Clinton!

FRANK (*disappearing*). Prove it.

,

JOE. You know what, fuck him. Right?

MEL. Sure.

JOE. Anyway, we get that story? No way he isn't gonna print it.

MEL. Did we just hear the same conversation?

JOE. Fine, so we take to a different newspaper.

MEL. And breach our contracts. Believe me, I wish I was a
happy little helium balloon like you, but I have alimony
payments like you wouldn't believe.

JOE. You think you'll have trouble getting *hired* after a story like that?

MEL. We don't have an address, we don't even know if this guy is still alive. I think this is an appropriate moment to admit defeat, don't you?

JOE. We should resign, that's what we should do.

MEL. Joey, this new Nancy Drew thing you have going on, it's adorable, but –

JOE. This is censorship, what's happening here, what you're / endorsing –

MEL. You've lost the patient, Joey! Stop the heart massage!

JOE. I haven't lost anything, you seem to have lost your fucking balls somewhere, but I haven't lost / anything –

MEL. You ever consider buying a new shirt, you know, one that's not made of hair? Try the Gap – because it *is* a shirt, Joe, it's fucking *costumery*, I can't believe I let you drag me all over five fucking boroughs with this shit. 'America must be shown!' Shown what? That some guy who took a great picture twenty-three years ago finally completed his difficult second album? You think you helped *make* that man? Bull*shit*, point and click, that's all *you* did, now you're trying to recycle an old photograph and call it a crusade, it's not a crusade, Joe, it's desperate masturbation, and I get my fill of that at home.

JOE. You're walking away from this so you can do what? Go back to your apartment to read your take-out menus, and your precious fucking first editions? Sniffing dust jackets, hoping you inhale some fucking talent, cos I tell you what, Mel, you might drink like Henry Miller, you might catch the clap like Henry Miller, but whatever your deluded fucking ego tells you, you sure as hell never wrote like him, cos unlike you, he understood the grey areas, / he –

MEL. You're a grey fucking area!

'

This isn't Watergate. This isn't Vietnam. You get your picture of Jimmy Wang, fifty, of Queens, and the fleeting attention it receives will only prove to you how inadequate you are.

JOE. Mel.

    ,

    Jesus.

    ,

MEL. I know. I know.

    Look at that. I did it, didn't I?

Scene Three

ZHANG LIN*'s apartment.* LIULI *climbs into the refrigerator and closes the door as* ZHANG LIN *enters with* DENG, *a prospective buyer. An efficient young businesswoman with an iPhone to her ear. She examines the refrigerator as* ZHANG LIN *watches. When she opens the door, the refrigerator is empty and clean. But* ZHANG LIN *cannot look at it.*

DENG (*Mandarin, on phone*). Yes. Yes. I'll ask him. (*To* ZHANG LIN.) Is it still in guarantee?

ZHANG LIN (*Mandarin*). No.

DENG (*Mandarin, on phone*). I'll call you back.

    She hangs up.

    Is there something wrong with it? I won't buy faulty goods.

ZHANG LIN. No, it works perfectly.

DENG. So why are you selling it?

    ,

ZHANG LIN. My wife doesn't like it.

    The sound of MING XIAOLI *coughing through the wall.*

DENG. She probably wants something more modern. Your walls are thin as ours.

ZHANG LIN. My neighbour.

DENG *looks round the back of the refrigerator.*

DENG. What's wrong with her?

ZHANG LIN. Have you looked out the window today? Look at that. I've been reading about it, the smog, it makes the blood sticky. Something about particles in the lungs.

DENG. I know, it's atmospheric.

ZHANG LIN. I don't think so.

DENG. You want to dust back here.

ZHANG LIN. I check the US Embassy website, they've got a monitor on their roof. Says it's at 540 today. The Party numbers never go above 200.

DENG. You think it's propaganda, is that it?

ZHANG LIN. No. I wasn't implying –

DENG. No but is that what you're trying to say, it's propaganda? It's not. These stories you've read, this stuff about the Embassy, that's propaganda, that's Americans trying to undermine us, our growth.

ZHANG LIN. I don't know. Maybe.

DENG. No, trust me, this is my business, I deal with this behaviour every day, only we call it corporate sabotage.

ZHANG LIN. You were wearing a face mask.

DENG. What's that?

ZHANG LIN. When you arrived. You were wearing a face mask.
'

DENG. Has this bulb been changed recently?

More coughing.

ZHANG LIN. She's fifty-nine.

DENG. Right, so the China she was born in was still medieval, thanks to the Party, she's going to die in a space age. She's a time traveller. She has motion sickness, is all.

MING XIAOLI*'s coughing becomes more racked.*

No, sounds nasty though. I'm sorry for her. There's no icebox?

ZHANG LIN. No.

DENG. I was really looking for something with an icebox, it's for my mother. I'll give you one hundred and fifty yuan.

ZHANG LIN. I was hoping for a little more.

DENG. When did you buy this?

ZHANG LIN. 1987. It was new then.

DENG. It's not new now, is it? One hundred and fifty yuan.

Scene Four

FRANK *in his office, phone in one hand, a dripping, oily jiffy bag in the other. Volcanic. Lights up on* JOE, *also on the phone, as he takes* FRANK*'s call.*

FRANK. Did you send me a fish?

JOE. Yes, Frank. Yes I did.

FRANK. You sent me a fucking – what the fuck is this?

JOE. A pollock, Frank. It's similar to cod.

FRANK. It's similar to me introducing your balls to my hunting knife. Doreen didn't get to it for two days, stunk my whole office out. I mean, Jesus! A pollock! You still pissed at me about pulling the Tank Man?

JOE. Yup.

FRANK. You wanna come in and talk about this?

JOE. Nope.

FRANK. Of course you don't, you know I'm still not gonna run it, right? I will *not* bow to terrorism, I hope you have this out of your system, because I want you and Mel in Boca Raton for the final debate and – Jesus H – DOREEN! Will you get in here? There's fish juice all over my desk, you remember who gave me this desk, Joe?

JOE. Henry / Kissinger.

> DOREEN *enters in rubber gloves. She takes the bag, exits with it at arm's length.*

FRANK. HENRY FUCKING KISSINGER. If you post me a fish again, I swear to God I will kill you and make it look like an accident.

Scene Five

ZHANG LIN*'s apartment.* ZHANG LIN *dressed in white.* ZHANG WEI *in his normal clothes. Wailing, off.* ZHANG LIN *is stuffing* MING XIAOLI*'s plant, now dead, into a bin bag.*

ZHANG LIN (*Mandarin*). Can you hear that?

ZHANG WEI (*Mandarin*). I can hear it, calm down.

ZHANG LIN. She can wail all she likes now. Her mother's dying, she can't get on a plane?

ZHANG WEI. It's a long way from San Francisco. She made it for the funeral.

ZHANG LIN. Sure, after Ming Xiaoli had been *dead* for two days.

> ZHANG LIN *goes to the window, gestures out.*

They say it's safe, look at it! I mean, what a miserable, what a really miserable way to – to be born on a farm, by the Yellow Sea –

ZHANG WEI. Poor.

ZHANG LIN. Yes poor, so what, poor, at least she could fucking breathe!

ZHANG WEI. Calm down. What happened to your fridge?

ZHANG LIN. Liuli wouldn't have allowed it, she would have been in there, every day!

ZHANG WEI. Zhang Lin, keep your voice down, where's your / fridge–

ZHANG LIN. I sold it. It made too much noise, all her old friends from the Party, checking their Rolexes, how long till lunch. You know how they bought them? With the shit from her lungs –

ZHANG WEI. You think the Party isn't looking into this? There are regulations, there / are rules –

ZHANG LIN. Oh, regulations, regulations, fantastic! No, that's wonderful, I'll make sure they put that on her memorial, 'Ming Xiaoli, dead of regulations'.

,

ZHANG WEI. When me and Yuanyuan were having trouble, she signed us up for this marriage counsellor, he made us write down all the things that were making us angry.

ZHANG LIN. Did it help?

ZHANG WEI. Yes. That's why we got divorced.

,

ZHANG LIN. Okay. I'll do that then.

ZHANG WEI. Okay. Good.

,

ZHANG LIN. I could send it to Joe.

ZHANG WEI. No, that's not / what I –

ZHANG LIN. I won't get it printed here, but the American press would be interested, right?

ZHANG WEI. Let's go next door, come on, pay / your respects.

ZHANG LIN. Joe would, anyway, Ming Xiaoli, she was on a poster, you know, poster girl for the Party, now she's dead because of, what? Because all they give a shit about is *growth*? That's a joke –

ZHANG WEI. You're upset, you mustn't / rush into anything.

ZHANG LIN *grabs his laptop, opens it, starts it up.*

ZHANG LIN. Through cooperation the electric light was fixed!

ZHANG WEI. My boss is in there. I have to show my face. Come and eat something, at least.

LIULI *emerges from the bin bag.* ZHANG LIN *sees her.* ZHANG WEI *does not. She proffers* ZHANG LIN *a peach.*

ZHANG LIN. I'll eat when I'm done.

ZHANG WEI. No, don't do anything!

Zhang Lin? Are you listening to me?

ZHANG LIN *doesn't answer.* ZHANG WEI *goes out.* ZHANG LIN *looks at* LIULI. *Many* LIULIS *enter. Red dresses flood the stage.* ZHANG LIN *is surrounded by them.* ZHANG LIN *begins to type. We keep sight of him, typing quickly, as, thousands of miles away:*

Scene Six

JOE, *without his camera, outside the Metropolitan Opera House. He's waiting. Cordoned off from a red carpet. A frenzy of camera flashes.* MARIA DUBIECKI *enters, with* DAVID. MARIA *is wearing an exquisite ball gown.* DAVID *is in black tie.* JOE *waves to* MARIA.

JOE. Hi, Maria! Maria, over here!

MARIA. Joe! Good to see you, you remember Dave, right?

DAVID. David. David Barker.

JOE. Hey. So that's a hell of a gown. Beethoven doesn't stand a chance tonight.

MARIA. These galas, I don't even know who half of these people *are*, I was going to pretend I had pink eye but Dave here basically got down on his knees and *begged* me, he wants to meet the Dixie Chicks – so listen, what happened, Frank demote you to the gossip column?

JOE. Nah, I was in the area, just wanted to say good luck. For next week.

MARIA. Luck? Honey, it'll be over by Iowa. Romney's about to get crushed by binderfuls of women. Good to see you, Joe.

MARIA makes to go. JOE hesitates. Then:

JOE. Wait a sec, while I have you, I'm trying to trace someone. His name is Jimmy Wang. He donated three hundred dollars to Senator Clinton's campaign / back in '08 –

MARIA. *Three hundred dollars?* Joe, I hope this doesn't sound self-important but: you know I'm kind of a big deal, don't you?

JOE. Just, come on, Maria, just help me out, will you?

MARIA. It's protected information, you know that.

JOE. I know. I just thought –

MARIA. Yeah, I know, you thought wrong, don't worry about it –

JOE. Look. I didn't want to do this but. But, okay, I have this colleague. And he has these files.

A beat. MARIA covers her panic beautifully, turns to DAVID with a dazzling smile.

MARIA. Dave, would you check my wrap? Thank you so much.

DAVID *hesitates.*

DAVID. I think it's going to rain. Your hair will go flat.

MARIA (*smiling*). Dave, honey, will you just check the wrap, okay?

DAVID *goes.* MARIA *turns to* JOE, *hisses.*

What you talking about, Joe, what *colleague*?

JOE. You wouldn't know him. But he's a big fan of yours, we both are, and what we're concerned about, Maria, is… well, people remember pictures like that. The smell of them hangs around.

Shouts of 'Maria!', from off, she turns, smiles, waves as she speaks.

MARIA. I don't know what you're talking about –

JOE. I'm talking about you wearing nothing but a Nixon T-shirt snorting cocaine off a cheerleader's wrist.

,

MARIA. Hey, we all have *pasts*, right!

JOE. Obama still keeping that Secretary of Education seat warm for you, by the way?

A tiny beat. MARIA *moves much closer to* JOE. *She keeps a fixed smile on her face.*

MARIA. There's a hurricane coming. I hope she picks you up and drops you in the fucking Hudson.

JOE. Come on, don't be like that.

MARIA. I thought you were a nice man, Joe.

,

JOE. I am. Jimmy Wang. W-A-N-G. You can reach me here whenever you're ready.

JOE *hands her a card. She takes it. Slips it into her clutch. Shouts from off of 'Maria! Maria!' Camera flashes firing as she smiles dumbly into the lenses, and* JOE *slinks off into the night.*

Scene Seven

ZHANG LIN, *still typing.* ZHANG WEI *standing behind him. Music playing through the laptop. It is 'Ode to Joy' from Beethoven's Ninth.*

ZHANG WEI (*Mandarin*). What are you doing, Zhang Lin? What are you doing?

ZHANG LIN (*Mandarin*). Stop bothering me.

ZHANG WEI. What are you writing? What does it say?

ZHANG LIN. How much do the pollution inspectors fine you?

ZHANG WEI. I don't know, not much, about six thousand – don't do this. Please don't do this – (*Points.*) why are you writing about him, you know who that is?

ZHANG LIN. He's a Party Official, he's looking into the smog.

ZHANG WEI. Okay but don't use his name, he owns my factory! Let's just, stop and, think about this, have a beer, do you want a beer?

ZHANG LIN. No. What year was Ming Xiaoli born?

ZHANG WEI. How the hell should I know! Please, Zhang Lin, don't.

LIULI. 1953.

ZHANG WEI. What's this word? Zhang Lin, what's this word you keep using, that one, there? And there, you better not be mentioning me, what does that mean?

ZHANG LIN. It's nothing to do with you.

ZHANG LIN *finishes. Leans back.*

It just means 'blood'.

ZHANG LIN *hits send.*

Black.

Interval.

ACT FOUR

Scene One

Lights up on PETER ROURKE *at his desk in Silicon Valley.
The CEO of Mytel computer systems, a US company with an
office in Beijing. He's typing, headphones on. Perhaps we hear
the music he's listening to. His secretary,* DAWN, *enters. He
looks up, pulls the headphones out.*

DAWN. Peter? I've been buzzing you. Judy's on line two / and –

PETER. Lawyer Judy or wife Judy?

DAWN. Lawyer Judy.

PETER. Got it.

> *He picks up the phone. Lights up on* JUDY, *in pyjamas and
> dressing gown.* DAWN *exits.*

> Hey, Judy Tuesday! How you all doing out there in
> Manhattan, you battening down the hatches?

JUDY. I'm not in the office, I've been working from home
Upstate this past month.

PETER. You take it easy on the East Coast, don't you?

JUDY. I had a heart attack, Peter.

PETER (*appalled*). Fuck. Judy, I'm so –

JUDY. I'm fine, Pete, I need to run something by you before I
authorise it. The Beijing office has a request for some detail
on a Chinese citizen.

> *Lights up on* ZHANG LIN. *His apartment is being searched
> by* SECURITY MEN.

PETER. Uh. Okay. He been a naughty boy?

JUDY. He posted an article online. Something about Party
corruption over the smog in Beijing. It went through an
anonymiser site but the Party picked it up.

PETER. He was using one of our systems?

JUDY. I didn't just call to hear your voice.

PETER. Okay, so what do they want? IP address I guess?

JUDY. And the location of the corresponding PC used to send it.

PETER. Dumb question: do we have any assurance as to what this data will be used for?

JUDY. You want the extended disco version again or –

PETER. Humour me.

JUDY (*sighs*). As a US company operating on Chinese soil you are required to comply with Chinese law. There's no assurance.

Peter? This is really just a courtesy –

PETER. Okay. Okay. Fine.

JUDY. I can give the clearance?

PETER. Yep. Sure.

ZHANG LIN's *laptop is seized.* ZHANG LIN *is handcuffed, and dragged out.*

JUDY. Okay. See you Saturday.

PETER. What's that?

JUDY. Company paintballing? I'm flying in Friday, I'm at the Fremont if you want me.

PETER. Okay well, see you then. Safe trip.

PETER *hangs up, lights down on* JUDY. PETER *stares at his desk, shaken. Then calls off:*

Dawn! Get in here!

DAWN *comes in.*

Judy had a heart attack.

DAWN (*puts a hand to her mouth*). Oh my God.

PETER. I know, right?

PETER *puts his headphones back in and starts typing again.*

Scene Two

ZHANG LIN *and a* PSB GUARD *in a Beijing interview room, sitting at a table. The* GUARD *wears Nike trainers. He is writing. A long pause as he does so. Without looking up:*

GUARD. Do you want to get tuberculosis?

ZHANG LIN. What am I being accused of?

The GUARD *hands him a written statement.*

GUARD. This is our first meeting. If there is a second, it won't be in a nice room like this. It will be, lying on bunks with old men. Coughing and sneezing.

ZHANG LIN. I didn't do anything.

GUARD. I thought you were a teacher.

ZHANG LIN. I am. I've taught the children of many / of your superiors –

GUARD. I thought teachers were smart. Sign just here.

,

ZHANG LIN. I didn't put my name on it. The article, I didn't put my name / on the –

GUARD. You know how easy it is to get that information? One phone call to New York.

ZHANG LIN. It was only online for six hours before it was firewalled.

GUARD. Chinese law states it is illegal to incite unrest.

,

ZHANG LIN. I'm sorry. I wasn't thinking straight. My neighbour is dead.

GUARD. The Party extends its sympathies. Sign, please. And the date.

,

Or have I made a mistake? You did send this article to a foreign journalist, correct?

ZHANG LIN. He didn't publish it. He wasn't able to – he said the story was too small, and the Americans can't even solve their own problems, they –

GUARD. There's no problem here. This part I've underlined, what does that say?

The GUARD *shows* ZHANG LIN *a copy of his article.*

ZHANG LIN. It says the smog was at 801 –

GUARD. The fog.

ZHANG LIN. I'm sorry?

GUARD. You mean the fog.

ZHANG LIN. Yes, the fog was at 801.

GUARD. But that's wrong, isn't it?

ZHANG LIN. Yes.

GUARD. Yes, it's wrong. Because the scale doesn't go beyond 500.

ZHANG LIN. Yes. What happened was, I was looking at an American website, and it said the smog was at that level, but –

GUARD. The fog.

ZHANG LIN. The fog was at that level but –

GUARD. But this information was incorrect?

ZHANG LIN. Yes, the fog was below 500.

GUARD. It was well below that. The readings for the time show levels of around 190.

ZHANG LIN. Yes, I'm sorry, it was a mistake, a stupid. I would like to apologise –

    ,

    I would like to apologise for the mistake. Please. Please. I won't –

GUARD. The same foreign journalist has been emailing you seditious material.

ZHANG LIN. That was, a mistake too.

GUARD. Lots of mistakes, eh? You think China would be a
better place, without jobs, without industry?

ZHANG LIN. No.

GUARD. You prefer the economy to fail?

ZHANG LIN. No. No, I was only pointing out that the sm– the
fog is, the fog is, it's a problem.

GUARD. It's not a problem. It's weather.

Beat. The GUARD *looks down at the article. Reads from it.*

This is a nice part: 'Somewhere in Beijing tonight, a woman
dies a third-world death in a new-world China built on her
sweat, and her blood, and her sacrifice. And across the city,
an official scratches his belly in his sleep, and dreams of
regulations…'

'

You see, I don't understand your complaint. Because you
say, right here, you say the Party has made regulations, so –

ZHANG LIN. No. I said dreams. Dreams of regulations.

GUARD. Cos dreams aren't real things, right?

ZHANG LIN. No, they're real. They're just subject to
interpretation.

'

GUARD. God, I hate English teachers. The Party takes
pollution very seriously. There are regulations. There are
inspections. Nobody is exempt. Sign.

ZHANG LIN. I could write a retraction of the article. Would
that help? Because I could do that –

GUARD. It's too late for retractions. Stand up.

ZHANG LIN *stands. The* GUARD *takes out a pen, hands it
to* ZHANG LIN.

Sign it.

ZHANG LIN *hesitates.*

It's only a statement. I'm trying to help you.

ZHANG LIN. Help me how?

GUARD. Help you to be happy.

,

LIULI *enters. The* GUARD *does not see her.*

ZHANG LIN. I read a study recently. A scientific study, it claimed that the happiest people are the ones who are best at lying to themselves. For example, an athlete who believes, truly believes, there's no one faster than him, is happy. Even if he comes last every time, he's still happy.

GUARD. Is there a point to this?

ZHANG LIN. Yes. I think you are a happy man.

The GUARD *surveys* ZHANG LIN. *Then with great deliberation, he puts out his cigarette, takes the statement from the table, folds it, puts it in his pocket. Takes the pen from* ZHANG LIN, *replaces the cap.*

GUARD. Take off your shoes.

Scene Three

JOE*'s apartment. The night of the 2012 Presidential election. The roses, now dead.* JOE, *watching the coverage as it's streamed through his laptop.* TESS, *off. They've been drinking.*

JOE. Tess! Get in here! They just called Ohio.

A toilet flushes, off. TESS *enters.*

TESS. It's over?

JOE. Not yet, it's just Fox. Wait for a proper news channel to call it.

JOE's cell rings. JOE *grabs it, looks at it, puts it down again, disappointed.*

Frank. He's having some big election party.

TESS. You didn't want to go?

JOE. Wine and cheese with a hundred people who voted for the other guy? That sound like a fun night to you? You going to show me your thing or what?

TESS. How dare you.

JOE (*laughs*). Your thing, your presentation, that's the whole / reason you came over.

TESS. Yeah, I know! Wait a second, okay. Okay.

She pulls on a pair of high heels. Takes her position. Holds an imaginary clicker. Takes a breath.

Okay so – I've got a whole PowerPoint thing, this is just – that's my clicker. So. Thank you all for coming here today. Hello, Cleveland!

,

She waits for him to laugh. He doesn't.

JOE. Sorry – you're doing this in Cleveland? / Only –

TESS. No, it's – *Spinal Tap*, I thought, start with / a –

JOE. Lose it.

TESS. Okay. Okay so… where was I… (*Sotto.*) 'Thank you for coming here today…'

Pause.

Shit. I had the whole thing memorised. Don't – it isn't *funny*! I actually have to do this in, in, in – (*Looks at her wrist.*) where's my watch gone – in, in the morning, stop laughing! I have to start drinking water.

JOE*'s buzzer sounds, he rushes to the intercom.*

JOE. Hello?

Perhaps we hear a muffled voice, perhaps JOE says 'come up'. JOE opens the door. Adrenaline racing. TESS kicks off the heels.

Okay. Okay. Give me some of that.

JOE takes the water from TESS. DAVID enters. He sees TESS, looks at JOE.

Hi, David. This is my friend, Tess.

DAVID. Pleased to meet you, Tess. I'm David, David Barker.

TESS. Hello.

,

TESS *looks at* JOE. JOE *closes the laptop*.

I might just step out for a cigarette.

DAVID. Thank you so much. Appreciate it.

TESS *steps out, takes a bottle of water.* DAVID *remains very still, looking at* JOE.

JOE. You want a – you want to take a drink or something?

DAVID. No. There's a party at the Sheraton. I have a cab waiting, I can't absent myself for too long. Senator Dubiecki doesn't know I'm here, if she ever speaks to you again, I'd be grateful if you didn't mention my visit.

,

JOE. Sorry, I don't –

DAVID. Look, I'm only someone's assistant so I'm sure you don't give a damn for what I have to say, but I've just been asked to meet you outside your apartment tomorrow, charged with a task I very much resent, and I've drunk half a bottle of champagne, so I'm going to say it anyway. Maria's not a perfect woman but she was born to a pair of immigrants in the back of a Ford Sedan and now she's a Senator, and she represents the interests of nearly twenty million people. And she represents them very well, for the most part. I don't know fully what your interests are here, but I'm guessing they are not shared by twenty million people. I'm guessing they're purely individual concerns. I know what you do, I know who you are –

JOE. You don't know / anything about me –

DAVID. I know your *type*. And there is nothing in your dwarf grasp you could hope to achieve in a lifetime that comes close to what that woman achieves in a single working week. So I hope that's something you can tango with during your more introspective moments, if indeed you have them, because I sure as hell couldn't.

,

JOE. Are you finished? Because –

DAVID. Four p.m., downstairs. If you're late I won't wait.

DAVID leaves.

TESS (*off*). Can I come in?

JOE. Yeah.

TESS enters. JOE fills a coffee mug with champagne, downs it. TESS grins.

TESS (*German accent*). Augustus, sweetheart, save some room for later!

JOE. What?

They both look up as distant, drunken voices become audible, singing 'The Star-Spangled Banner'. The sound of fireworks. JOE opens his laptop. They sit, watching. Presently:

(*Quiet.*) He got it. Four more years.

TESS. What about Florida?

JOE. Doesn't matter. He doesn't need it.

,

TESS. I wonder what it'll mean.

JOE. It means I never have to take another shot of Romney reflected in a pair of Ray-Bans.

,

I don't feel anything. Do you feel anything?

TESS (*yawns*). Bit pissed.

,

Do you owe money to the mob?

JOE. What?

TESS. That man, / what did he –

JOE. I think people need to know that there is heroism in the world, don't you?

TESS. Oh yeah. Definitely.

JOE. That's in the interest of people, right?

TESS. Absolutely.

JOE. No, but a lot of people. Like, more than twenty million? To see a picture of, just a normal man. Who stood up, and for that not to be a desolate thing, not a martyr, who can give a shit about martyrs these days, but a normal man who survived, carried on, made a life –

TESS. It's the sun and the wind.

JOE. Right, thank you. What?

TESS. The man. With the coat, how d'you make a man take his / coat off?

JOE. Right. Thank you, and that's not, I mean how is that masturbation?

TESS. It's completely not.

JOE. Because the other way doesn't work. You can't shock anyone into anything, not any more –

TESS *lights a cigarette*.

Not when kids queue up at the movies to watch some guy who gets his kicks throwing teenagers into pits of needles, or sewing them mouth-to-asshole –

TESS. I saw that one.

She shudders.

JOE. Right, or whatever, so what's horror? Just, just something we watch, just a, milky thrill, a titillation –

TESS. Clip art. Fucking clip art.

JOE. Exactly. Exactly, the effect is gone. The shock is… too familiar so, so so I'm just looking for a, a different angle. A different kind of picture. Not of darkness, but light. I think that could be a, a *good* thing. I'm not trying to hurt anybody –

TESS. You're not going to hurt anybody. Look at you, you're a shrimp, you couldn't hurt anybody.

JOE. That's what I'm saying, I don't want to.

TESS. Then don't.

JOE kisses TESS. She pulls away. Then kisses him. They begin to make love.

Scene Four

The Beijing interview room. ZHANG LIN tied to a chair. No shoes, no shirt. Lash wounds on his feet and torso. Mouth stuffed with rags. Two GUARDS. Electrodes attached to his toes. Shocks are now administered. The chair shakes with the jolting of ZHANG LIN's body.

Scene Five

JOE's apartment. JOE and TESS in a crumpled heap on the floor, under a blanket. A few hours later. JOE watches TESS sleeping. Gently shakes her. She stirs, sees him.

JOE. Hey.

TESS. Hey.

JOE. Just you said you had an early start.

TESS. I did?

JOE. I'd offer you breakfast, only we already drank it.

He grins, picks up an empty champagne bottle.

TESS. No, that's –

JOE. I can call you a cab, if you like?

> ,

TESS. No. I can walk.

JOE. Just my wife'll be home soon.

> JOE *smiles*. TESS *laughs. Too loudly.*

> Wasn't that funny.

TESS. No, no I was just thinking. I bet they normally go for that line, don't they?

> ,

JOE. Come on, I wasn't – I'm not.

> TESS *starts to dress.* JOE *watches her, uncertain and self-conscious.* TESS *looks around.* JOE *reaches for something on the sofa, hands her bra to her. She takes it, quickly.*

TESS. It's okay, Joe! I know the drill, you have a morning, I have a morning, I'll just, shoes, bag, out the door, I won't even ask to borrow a toothbrush, because that's always mortifying, isn't it? Someone looking at their watch while you floss –

> TESS *pulls on her trainers. Grabs her bag.*

JOE. Tess, wait a second –

TESS. No, it's fine, just give me a minute, I'll be out of your hair.

> TESS *checks she has everything and heads for the door.*

JOE. Can I buy you dinner?

TESS. Yeah, great! Call me.

JOE. Can you. Just.

> Stop – I'm trying to. I mean it, I'd like to see you tonight. In fact, since I've known you I, well I've wanted to see you most nights, which is, that's a little… new for me, so. So I have this dinner, with Zhang Lin's nephew, Benny, why don't you come? It's this steak place, Peter Luger's, in Williamsburg. Seven thirty, we'll have dinner with Benny, put him in a cab then –

TESS. I hate Williamsburg.

JOE. Of course you do. It's an awful place. Vintage clothing stores and, and, and… brunch, but it's just a couple hours, tops, then we'll get right back on the L train / and –

TESS. I got mugged on the L train.

JOE. Then we will take a cab, come on. Let me buy you a steak.

TESS. I'm a vegetarian.

JOE (*grins*). The hell you are.

He kisses her.

Scene Six

ZHANG LIN*'s apartment.* ZHANG LIN *sits or lies, covered with a blanket, very ill. In great pain. He retches into a bowl.* ZHANG WEI *is bathing his feet.*

ZHANG WEI (*Mandarin*). Where does it hurt?

ZHANG LIN (*Mandarin*). It hurts everywhere.

I'm so sorry. Zhang Wei, I'm so sorry I'm so –

ZHANG WEI. They let you go.

ZHANG LIN. I don't want to make trouble for you –

ZHANG WEI. Don't worry about me, I'm fine. If they'd put you on a surveillance list you'd know about it by now.

ZHANG LIN *makes a sound in pain.*

Shh. It's alright. You're safe. You said your piece. And she would've been proud of you, you know that? I'm proud of you too but you don't have to prove anything to anyone. Things can go back to normal now, it'll be easier than you think.

'

We need more iodine. I won't be long. I'll put the TV on. Okay?

ZHANG WEI *puts the TV on. WEI leaves. ZHANG LIN turns off the TV. Grasps for his laptop. Picks up the microphone.*

Lights up on LIULI *and* YOUNG ZHANG LIN *in Tiananmen Square. The 3rd of June. A polystyrene Statue of Liberty being erected in the background. Music. A sense of an excitable, jubilant crowd. 'Ode to Joy' playing on a distant speaker system.*

LIULI. What's the time?

YOUNG ZHANG LIN. Nearly ten thirty. You want to leave?

LIULI *shakes her head.*

LIULI. We've taken the square. The city belongs to us.

YOUNG ZHANG LIN *lights a cigarette. Surveys the square. Conversational.*

YOUNG ZHANG LIN. They're bringing the Army in now.

LIULI. So? The People's Army.

YOUNG ZHANG LIN. No, I know.

,

LIULI. You remember all those boys from school? Sun Ho and Wang Pengfei and Li Fu-Han, showing off their uniforms. Stupid boys with shiny buttons.

YOUNG ZHANG LIN. And little Qiu Hong Wen who couldn't grow a moustache.

They laugh. Observe. Pause.

YOUNG ZHANG LIN. They're pushing forward.

LIULI. There's too many of us.

,

YOUNG ZHANG LIN. You look tired. Maybe we should think about –

LIULI. We haven't got what we came for, not yet.

,

YOUNG ZHANG LIN. Are you cold?

LIULI. No.

,

YOUNG ZHANG LIN. You look cold.

LIULI. I'm not.

,

YOUNG ZHANG LIN. Maybe. Just to be on the safe side.

LIULI. They're just here for show!

YOUNG ZHANG LIN. But there's a small chance they might –

LIULI. Rubber bullets you said.

YOUNG ZHANG LIN. You're pregnant.

LIULI. And?

YOUNG ZHANG LIN. And a pregnant woman shouldn't risk getting hit with bullets.

LIULI. Rubber bullets.

YOUNG ZHANG LIN. Any bullets.

He puts out his cigarette.

Let's go.

LIULI. Shh – do you hear that?

YOUNG ZHANG LIN. It's the tanks moving. The buses are burning, they're trying to get round.

LIULI *stares off. An approaching sound of a crowd, panicking.* YOUNG ZHANG LIN *looks. Alarm. He tries to remain calm, steer her away.* LIULI *twists from him. Mesmerised.*

LIULI. Why are they running?

YOUNG ZHANG LIN. I don't know.

LIULI. Why are they running?

YOUNG ZHANG LIN. I don't know. Let's go.

LIULI. I want to go home.

YOUNG ZHANG LIN. That's good –

LIULI. Why is everyone running?

*Snap blackout. Gunfire. Feet on concrete, screams, the
shouts of the Army, a crowd panicking. Then sound and
vision cut out. It's quiet and dark. Lights up on* ZHANG
LIN, *weeping, wretched.* ZHANG WEI *enters. Rushes to his
brother.* ZHANG LIN *grasps at him.*

ZHANG WEI. It's alright. It's alright. I'm here. It's all over now.

ZHANG LIN. No. I don't think so. My feet. Zhang Wei, / my
feet sting.

ZHANG WEI. Shh. Go to sleep.

ZHANG LIN. I don't want to go to sleep. I don't want to go to
sleep.

Scene Seven

TESS *is mid-speech, before her PowerPoint presentation, a
clicker in her hand.*

TESS.…so we're late to the party, the road to the Chinese
market is already well-trodden, and you know what? It's
littered with the corpses of companies who blithely assumed
that Chinese consumers would bite off their hands for
anything America wanted to hawk to them. Disney, Mattel,
Groupon, eBay, Nestlé, these are not chicken-feed mom-and-
pop operations. They're multinational businesses, who've
put vast resources into researching the Chinese market. And
they've all failed. Because they believed China was looking
over the fence wanting to *be* America and nothing could be
further from the truth.

What about the good-news stories? Starbucks, McDonald's,
KFC? There's no magic ingredient in their coffee, their
burgers, their buckets of chicken, their success lies in the fact
they made themselves Chinese enough in a country that
values the supremacy of its culture above all else. You can

have congee for breakfast at The Savoy. You walk into Givenchy or Hermès in Paris, the staff speak Mandarin, because those companies understand that China is not the drunk girl at the frat party. She's the business major with an A-plus average, and really great hair. She's in charge of this brave new economic world, you bend to her or you die trying.

And how are those Chinese tourists paying for their room service, their ostrich-skin handbags? Not with our cards, or the cards of our rivals, even, but with the, singular, state-sponsored card, UnionPay. How do we change this? We can't, not unless we understand the Chinese consumer. Which is where I come in.

What I'm about to show you is a portfolio of seven customer segments. We'll get into the variations in a minute, but they're united by one thing. They love to shop. We have to abandon the myth that China is a nation of savers with no interest in credit cards. Because it is a myth, the only way the Chinese are different to us is they make sure they have the money before they spend it, but they do spend it. We only have to look at this picture to know that:

TESS *clicks, the Tank Man photograph appears.*

What is this an image of? Protest, of course, but more than that, this is a picture of the moment that China exchanged democracy for an economic miracle. For the opportunity to work, live, spend, progress. Aspire – and credit cards live and die on aspiration or desperation – so this is a photograph of the moment that our mission went from being unthinkable, to being tantalisingly *possible*. And then, of course, all we had to do was wait another twenty-three years for them to let us in! By the way, can I point out:

TESS *clicks. Two red circles appear around his shopping bags. She turns back to us.*

The Tank Man… has been shopping! One of the most iconic images to come out of China, and at its heart a man who's just been to the store, to buy, what? Rice, a newspaper, socks, dried…

,

…dried duck stomach, whatever.

TESS *is becoming less sure of herself; her voice wavers. She clicks. The first archetype appears.*

So, let's look at the segments. The first one I'm calling 'The Rural Dreamer'. They're often in their thirties, sorry, late teens to mid-twenties. They have, they have a high brand awareness, but minimal free time, and much of their money is sent home, a high brand awareness, they –

TESS *clicks on to the next one by mistake. Her hands are shaking.*

Oh, whoops, sorry, I just – Jaydene? How do I – is there a back button or something?

She looks out, lost. Trying to remain breezy.

Sorry, just I double-clicked, I'm still on the Rural Dreamer, I'm not sure how to –

Jaydene? Any joy?

Pause.

Well, that's okay, okay… okay… okay so, so let's talk about, 'The Luddite Shopper' instead, seeing as we're – okay, the Luddite Shopper. The Luddite Shopper is. It's (Jesus), it's the Rural Dreamer with a different picture on it.

Pause.

The Luddite – sorry, actually, these categories are. These categories are, well, for a start, these categories are, they're just versions of Western categories. Which is, it's what you asked for but. But I need five years to build a really accurate segmentation and, well, you have me on a six-month contract. And I'm used to that, that's business cycles, right, but China's moving faster than we can collect the data, I mean, this is a nation that's gone from famine to Slim-Fast in one generation. I know some of you've been out there, I mean, did you see the *smog*? My last trip, it rained one day, the puddles were black, the sky was yellow, they're growing so fast you can see it in the air! And, you know, in the fact there are like thousands of babies who can't breathe properly, but anyway, they've had, what? Forty years' worth of economic evolution in the last ten years and that's, you know, amazing but actually, that's not, it's not a safe speed to be moving at.

Because and also, I mean, I'm sorry if this is – but have we really thought about what happens when you turn one-point-three billion economic pragmatists into people who think about money like *us*? I mean, we're still breaking our nails on a recession now, right? But, what is it going to be *like* if one-point-three *billion* Chinese renege on their mortgages and credit-card payments?

And you know, this isn't me trying to tell you that the dog ate my homework, this work, it's fine, it's rushed but it's fine, it'll get you over the finishing line before American Express, but then what? Because you're about to get into bed with someone you don't really understand which is, it just seems a bit… lunatic, because, you know, this is the future. It's the next hundred years. And we don't understand. And I think that might a problem. Right?

The image behind her skips back to the Tank Man photograph. TESS *glances at it.*

Thanks, Jaydene, that's – yep. I've got it now.

Scene Eight

Outside JOE*'s apartment.* JOE *has been waiting here for a very long time. He has an A4 envelope on his lap and is smoking.* DAVID *enters, wheeling his bike which has a baby seat on the back and saddlebags. His cycle helmet unclipped, he wears a suit with a fluorescent jacket, bicycle clips. One trouser knee is ripped open, a bloody bandage around it.*

JOE. You said four p.m.! I've been sitting out here three hours, you couldn't call?

DAVID. I'm so sorry to hear that.

DAVID *kicks down the stand on his bicycle.*

JOE. It's fine, I just. I have to be in Brooklyn in twenty minutes –

DAVID. You have something for me to collect?

JOE. Right, sure, I have it right here.

DAVID. This is the only copy?

JOE. Yeah. The negatives are in there too.

> JOE *gives him the envelope, unsealed.* DAVID *glances inside.*

DAVID. Do you have a pen?

> JOE *quickly takes out his pen and a notepad.*

One twelve 169th Street, Queens.

JOE. Work or home?

DAVID. He lives above the shop.

> DAVID *kicks up the stand on his bike.*

JOE. Listen, David, about what you said, last night. I. I've been thinking about it a lot and, well, I wanted to say. It's not my fault you've got no fucking imagination.

> *Beat.* DAVID *goes.* JOE *examines the address. This precious information. Checks his watch. Takes out his phone, makes a call, scanning the street. He is feverish with excitement.*

Shit. (*He's connected.*) Hi, Tess, I'm going to be like, ten minutes late, I just, I have an errand to run but I hope your thing went well and. And I can't wait to see you. It's Joe, by the way. And I can't wait to see you, I said that, didn't I, okay, bye –

> *He hangs up, flings out his arm –*

Taxi!

Scene Nine

Outside the Glorious City Flower Shop. PENGSI is closing up for the day. JOE enters, excited and flushed.

JOE. Jimmy Wang.

PENGSI. Closed. Sorry. Tomorrow / at eight a.m., we open –

JOE. Your name is Jimmy Wang, right?

PENGSI. No.

JOE. No, it's okay. It just – I need you to tell me the truth. Feng Meihui placed that ad for you. And she brought you here, didn't she? In '89, why did you take out that ad?

PENGSI. No, not me. Wrong man.

He shows PENGSI the Tank Man picture.

JOE. The man in this photo? It's you, isn't it?

PENGSI. You go now.

JOE. Please. I think you can help me. Jimmy Wang, is your real name Wang Pengfei?

PENGSI. YOU GO PLEASE.

PENGSI'S WIFE enters and speaks rapidly in Mandarin to her husband. He speaks back.

JOE. What was that? I heard you, I speak Mandarin, you said brother, your brother.

PENGSI. No.

JOE. I speak Mandarin – you did you said your brother and then –

PENGSI shouts in Mandarin at his WIFE, she runs out.

I'm just asking for a little cooperation here, I'm not –

PENGSI tries to push him out.

Is he your brother? This man, in the picture, he's your brother –

PENGSI starts to manhandle him, JOE is stronger. He shoves PENGSI against the wall. Jolts him a few times. PENGSI yells for help.

Shut up! Shhh just – be quiet okay?

PENGSI. Get off!

JOE. Just be quiet –

PENGSI. Fuck you. Get out my store.

JOE. Please –

> PENGSI *spits in his face*, JOE *reacts lightning quick, punches him in the face*, PENGSI *crumples*, JOE *hauls him up, shoves him to the wall*.

> I didn't mean to – that was a mistake, you shouldn't've, just tell me –

> PENGSI *swings for* JOE, *misses*, JOE *slams him onto the floor, holds him there*.

> Just tell me. Just tell me. I don't want to hurt you / just –

PENGSI. Please. My brother was…

JOE. Your brother was what?

> JOE *shakes him again*.

> Your brother was what?

PENGSI. Yes.

JOE. Yes what? The Tank Man?

PENGSI. Yes. Tank Man.

> *Pause*. JOE *releases* PENGSI. *Stumbles away. Holds his fist*.

JOE. Is he… is he okay? Is Wang Pengfei alive?

> PENGSI *shakes his head*, JOE *shows him the Tank Man photo again*.

> Are you sure? Look. This man, you're sure he's not –

PENGSI. I don't know about this man.

JOE. But you just said, he's your brother.

PENGSI. No, not my brother this man.

JOE. But you just / said –

PENGSI. Not my brother, this man.

JOE. You're not making sense!

PENGSI. The man… the tank…

JOE (*points*). This man.

PENGSI. No. (*Moves* JOE*'s finger.*) This man. Here. The soldier. In the tank, he was my brother. Unknown hero, my brother.

> PENGSI*'s wife runs in. Smashes* JOE *in the face with a wrench.* JOE*'s nose explodes in blood. He stumbles.* PENGSI'S WIFE *yells in Mandarin.* PENGSI *hollers back. She storms out.*

> She'll call the police! You go now.

> JOE *moves onto his knees, clutching his nose.*

JOE. You're illegal, she's not going to bring the cops here – ah, shit. Where is he now? Your brother?

,

PENGSI. He was executed.

JOE. But… he was a solider, why would they –

PENGSI. He never killed. He would not drive tank forward when someone was there.

JOE. Someone? You mean the man with the shopping bags?

PENGSI. Yes. He could not go round, so he would not go. The Party were angry. Everyone looks at the man. With the shopping bag. But here, you can see, very small, a man coming out. Then he disappear again. Inside the tank. And that man was my brother. And he was very brave.

> *Sirens, faint at first. Getting louder.* PENGSI'S WIFE *comes out, panicked and fearful. She says in Mandarin: 'Can you hear that! Can you hear that! It's her, next door, she called them!'*

JOE. She called them? They'll take you in! Why did she / do that –

PENGSI. Not her. Must be next door, a lady. Nosy on this block. We try to live quiet.

,

JOE. I – I'm sorry. I'm so sorry, I don't – here. Here, take this.

He takes out money, thrusts it at PENGSI. JOE *wipes blood from his nose. The sirens get louder. Blue and red lights flash across his face.*

Scene Ten

TESS, *dressed up, and* BENNY *sit in awkward silence in Peter Luger's steakhouse at a table for three. A* WAITER *enters, puts two steaks down in front of them and clears the cutlery from the third place.*

Scene Eleven

A Queens police station. JOE *comes out from the cells into the foyer. His nose is busted. He has a dressing splayed over it.* OFFICER HYTE *is escorting him.*

OFFICER HYTE. We have all we need from you. Bail's been posted so don't you go taking a winter cruise or anything now.

JOE (*looking about*). Where is she? Who posted my bail?

OFFICER HYTE. How should I know? I am not your concierge! Fucking night shift, you'll get your court date in a couple weeks. Should only be a fine if you're lucky.

JOE. Is he – was he legal?

OFFICER HYTE. Don't believe so. Won't affect your case, that's brought by the State of New York.

JOE. No but, will he be deported?

OFFICER HYTE. Depends. How good a lawyer you think he can afford?

OFFICER HYTE *goes as* FRANK *enters. He and* JOE *look at each other.*

FRANK. Nice nose-job. It hurt?

JOE. Little bit.

FRANK. Good.

,

JOE. You posted my bail?

FRANK. I did.

JOE. Well, / thanks, Frank. I really –

FRANK. You want to tell me why Senator Dubiecki's office called me and cancelled Jim and Heather's access to the press conference today?

JOE. Why would I know that?

FRANK. Because after Maria's office called, I called Maria. And Maria put me on *hold*, Joe. D'you know when I was last put on hold? I can't remember the time, I cannot actually remember, but Maria did it, she had me listening to Handel's fucking *Water Music* for a full eight minutes, and when I finally got through she was awful frosty with me, which, I couldn't understand it cos me and Maria, we have form, so I say to her 'What's this I'm hearing about the conference, why are my guys in the fucking ejector seats?', except I didn't curse, I was very calm, very breezy, but she wasn't, she was not breezy, fucking arctic *wind* coming down the line, and d'you know what she said to me? / Joe?

JOE. No.

FRANK. She said 'Ask your fuck-weasel photographer.' One of the most eloquent, elegant, orators of her generation, she uses the word 'fuck-weasel' and hangs up on me. Which is not, it doesn't happen to me a lot, so it resonated, so I'm thinking whatever it is, she's probably right. You are a fuck-weasel. So you're fired.

,

JOE. Oh by the way I rang your cell yesterday. It was so weird, Mary Chang picked up.

,

Mary Chang the stripper? Should be careful, I could've been Tina, / or the girls –

FRANK. I gave her a *job*, you little prick. I'm sponsoring her green card application, you didn't even give me her résumé when she / asked you –

JOE. Because I knew you wouldn't –

FRANK. *But I did.*

,

JOE. Well, I'm –

FRANK. What did you do to Maria, Joey? What the hell did you do?

JOE. I didn't do anything! I needed her help, she was resisting, I just… greased the… whatever. Look, okay, Frank / this is –

FRANK. It's the day after a fucking election, they kicked my embeds out! Do you understand what that means? Do you even get how many fires I'm fighting here? Joe, I hope your greasy whatever was worth it, because by the way, this is not me blowing off steam, this is it, you and I are finished, I free you from the terrible compromise of being employed by me, I hope you go fucking blind.

FRANK *goes as* OFFICER HYTE *returns with* JOE*'s wallet, keys, phone, etc. Hands them to* JOE, *as* TESS *enters.*

OFFICER HYTE. You left your stuff.

JOE. Thanks.

OFFICER HYTE *goes.* JOE *moves towards* TESS.

I'm so sorry.

Tess? I didn't mean to –

TESS. They brought them in while I was at the desk. They put them in a cell.

,

I just came to see if you were alright. And you are, so I'm, I'll go now.

JOE. I was coming, Tess, I meant to be there, things / just got –

TESS. Yes, I know. I listened to that voicemail you left, you sounded so, you were so excited. And I was excited too. I got fired today, but I didn't even care, not much, I came home, tried on dresses, stomach in knots, skipping down Broadway like some fucking cunt from a musical, and it took me all the time, how slow is this, all the time till I was sitting opposite Benny, in Williamsburg, holding a steak knife and understanding you weren't late, you just weren't coming, to realise: we were excited about completely different things.

JOE. That's not true. That's not true –

TESS. A photograph? Two people, destroyed, for that? What a bloody waste, I hope you find him, I do, but I am not… insignificant just because I never stepped in front of a fucking tank.

JOE. I know that.

TESS. Well, good. Anyway, I think. I think I'm in love with you. I think I have been for

well, quite a long time now. And it's nothing to do with… what you do, your work, my work isn't who I am, it's because, I think it's mostly just that I was scared, on a plane. And you held my hand. And you were very kind.

JOE *sits, hides his face.* TESS *stands over him. Pulls his hands from his face. He looks up at her. She runs her fingers over the scar by his eye.*

They made her take off her wedding ring. Jimmy Wang's wife. It was so awful, Joe. She screamed and screamed and screamed.

TESS *goes.* JOE *takes out his phone. Split scene with* ZHANG LIN, *in his apartment, as he answers the call.*

ZHANG LIN. Joe? Are you okay? Zhang Wei heard from Benny. He said you didn't show up to your dinner. He was very disappointed.

JOE. Yeah well, I'm disappointed too, that name you gave me, I found his brother.

ZHANG LIN. Really? How is he?

JOE. He's not the fucking Tank Man and he's not the fucking Tank Man's brother is how he is, Wang Pengfei was a solider, some soldier, some teenager who'd probably just spent two days gunning down civilians –

ZHANG LIN. He was a hero.

JOE. He's not a fucking hero, he was on the side of the Party, how / is that a –

ZHANG LIN. Sides? What does sides have to do with anything, he was a, he was a good man, even the Party saw that, you know how they used your picture? As a portrait of their humanity, look, we went around him! Did you know you were in the propaganda business? But it wasn't them, it was Wang Pengfei. And I don't know what happened to him.

JOE. His brother said he was shot.

,

ZHANG LIN. I'm sorry I wasted your time. I thought it was a good story. Sometimes a uniform makes it much harder to be a hero. And I thought you were interested in what happened that day.

JOE. I was interested in the Tank Man.

ZHANG LIN. Yes. I misunderstood.

,

JOE. I'm sorry about Benny. I'll call him. How are you?

ZHANG LIN. A new family moved into Ming Xiaoli's apartment. They have triplets.

JOE. Yeah, by the way, sorry about that I just, one old lady and some smog, I couldn't –

ZHANG LIN. She was only fifty-nine.

JOE. Okay, well. I, I'm kind of between things just now. You should come and visit.

ZHANG LIN. I wouldn't get a visa. And I don't have a work permit.

JOE. Well, I could help you out with that.

ZHANG LIN. Really?

JOE. Sure. I told you that, or, you know, we could just get married.

,

ZHANG LIN. I'll think about it.

ACT FIVE

Scene One

ZHANG LIN, *with a megaphone, addressing a crowd.*

ZHANG LIN. We call for a Party that refuses to get rich on our blood. We call for a Party that puts its people over its profits. We call for a Party that does not turn a blind eye as young men walk wheezing upstairs. We call for these things, at the top of our voices, while there is still breath in our lungs to do so.

Scene Two

April 2013. ZHANG LIN *and* ZHANG WEI. *Looking up at a security camera that has been mounted on the wall outside of* ZHANG LIN*'s apartment.* ZHANG WEI *is furious.*

ZHANG WEI (*Mandarin*). Do you see that?

ZHANG LIN (*Mandarin*). Yes, I've seen it. I'm sorry.

ZHANG WEI. What's wrong with you? My secretary saw you in the park!

ZHANG LIN. There were lots of other people there too.

ZHANG WEI. Did they all come home to find security cameras outside their homes?

ZHANG LIN. I'm sorry, Zhang Wei.

ZHANG WEI. I left the office, no one would even look me in the eye, felt like I was contagious or something.

ZHANG LIN. The Party won't hurt you.

ZHANG WEI. I wish they would, a beating, I could deal with a beating, that would be better than this, better than being unemployable for the rest of my fucking life. I won't get another job now, you know that, don't you? I'll have to leave the city.

ZHANG LIN. You could visit Benny. You'll get a visa no problem that way. Just tell them you're visiting Benny. Then it's the truth. Just make sure you pretend you're coming back.

ZHANG WEI. I can't live with people like that, you know the stuff they say about us? What about you? What are you going to do?

ZHANG LIN. I have Joe.

ZHANG WEI. Oh sure, the ghost who won't return your phone calls. Americans, they don't understand guanxi.

ZHANG LIN. That one does. I taught him. He asked me to marry him, did I tell you?

ZHANG WEI. I hope you got this off your chest, I hope it was worth it, to do that.

,

ZHANG LIN. We used to want the same things.

ZHANG WEI. Yes. I know we did. And then after, you took to your bed, like a little boy. And I went to work, like a man.

,

Call him again.

ZHANG LIN. I'll call him when I get in.

,

ZHANG WEI. Americans, I hate Americans. Their teeth are too white.

ZHANG WEI *goes.* ZHANG LIN *looks up into the security camera. He walks closer to it. Peering up into the lens. Framing his own close-up. Then he quietly takes out his camera phone, and takes a picture of the security camera.*

Scene Three

May 2013. Somewhere near a kettling, New York. TESS enters.
She appears to be crying, eyes streaming, but her manner,
though irritated, is not upset. She is six months pregnant but she
wears a tailored dress and jacket, and stiletto heels. She blinks
furiously, in pain.

TESS. jesuschristjesusfuckingchrist

She makes out the shape of JOE *but cannot see him with any*
clarity.

Excuse me? Excuse me? Could you give me a hand?

JOE, *absorbed in his camera, now a digital one, rather than*
the film camera we have seen him using, does not hear her.
She wipes her hand across her streaming eyes. Does a sharp
whistle, JOE *turns, sees her. Contemplates walking away.*
Does not.

JOE. Hey. Tess. Hey.

TESS. Who is that?

JOE. It's me, it's Joe –

TESS. Joe? As in… Joe?

JOE. Joe Schofield.

TESS. Oh my God –

He moves towards her, registers her pregnancy; her
streaming eyes.

JOE. What happened? Are you okay?

TESS. Oh, it's, no it's just pepper spray, I'm / fine –

JOE. Shit, you want some water –

TESS. No, you have to put milk on it – you never got pepper
sprayed?

She dumps her bags, pulls a carton of milk from the
shopping bag, tries to open it.

JOE. Only socially.

TESS. Here, help me out. Hang on –

She gives him the carton. JOE *rips it open,* TESS *takes off her jacket, rummages in her handbag, pulls out a rain poncho, shakes it out, pulls the poncho on over her head to protect her dress.*

JOE. Has this happened before?

TESS. Yeah, little bit. Okay. You can, you can pour it now.

TESS *leans back.* JOE *hesitantly pours the milk into her eyes, trying to steer clear of the bump.*

JOE. Does it sting?

TESS. It's pepper spray, Joe.

She laughs. JOE *takes her picture.*

Did you just take my picture?

JOE. Sorry. Force of habit. I thought you went back to England.

TESS. I got a stay of execution. Landed a new contract, Tesco, it's this British company, they set up over here, cocked the whole thing up, tried to sell packets of four rolls of loo paper when Americans want to buy forty at a time, that kind of basic, you know, total incompetence.

JOE. So what are you doing here?

TESS. This is just, it's a side project, it's extra-curricular. *Pro bono.* I'm helping them out, just a bit of basic profiling, improving their outreach.

JOE. You're working for a… multi-national corporation and an anti-capitalist protest?

TESS. Right.

JOE. Right. I mean, that's kind of schizophrenic –

TESS (*laughs*). Isn't it though! They can't work me out, it's hilarious.

'

JOE. Anyway. Congratulations.

TESS. For what?

JOE. The – the baby.

TESS. Oh, right, yep. Thanks.

JOE. What. I mean, what's that like?

TESS. It's okay. I had constant morning sickness for like, five months but my hair looks like a fucking Pantene advert so. You know, swings and roundabouts.

JOE. Do you think – I mean, is that safe? Being here?

TESS. Oh, the doctor says it's really got its feet under the table now. So how are you, you look well, are you well?

TESS *takes out a packet of gum, concentrates on retrieving a piece.*

JOE. Uh, yeah. Fine. Just, you know, I'm, I'm seeing someone, Heidi.

TESS. Uh-uh, that's great, you want some gum?

JOE. No thanks. She's a model. Not like, catwalk or anything. Hand model.

TESS. Oh, right. Sorry, what?

JOE. It's like a regular photographic model but only for jewellery, or nail polish.

TESS. Okay. That's. Has she got nice hands then?

JOE. Yeah, no they're… nice. Nice hands.

TESS. You live together?

JOE. Yeah. It's cheaper this way.

TESS. The four words every girl wants to hear! 'My darling… it's cheaper this way.'

'

No, but that's great! I'm really, good for you, so listen, you have an exhibition coming up, right? Howard Greenberg, very nice, I saw the poster.

JOE. Yeah. They approached me a couple years ago but I wasn't. I wasn't sure I wanted to, but now, / I'm –

TESS. Now you're broke.

JOE (*laughs*). Now I'm broke, right. No, I mean, I am but I also think that if it gets people to look at them then… the opening's next week, I'd love it if you, I mean if you could make it I would. I would love that. I can send you an invitation.

TESS. Yeah. Thanks. I'll see.

JOE. Because actually it's, I know the poster probably made it look all ritzy and all –

TESS. Sponsored by American Express.

JOE. Yeah, that's the gallery, that's not me, I mean I didn't –

TESS. Yeah but you're *in* the gallery, right? They didn't, like put a gun to your head, 'Show us your portfolio!'

JOE. No. No they didn't do that.

TESS. Do you get one of those big shiny coffee-table books?

JOE. I do. Give you one if you come.

TESS. Well. Yeah, send the invitation.

JOE. You can bring your… the father, I'd love to meet him.

A very long pause.

Oh. Oh. Right.

TESS. I did try to call you, I called… quite a few times, when / I –

JOE. Yeah, I know, I just. I went a little, after we. I went travelling. Round the country, for a. Long time, sorry, I'm just… I'm just…

,

TESS. I didn't want to leave some voicemail. And I knew your… position, you were very clear about that. And well I sort of thought I couldn't. Have them. I have a, well they call it a 'hostile environment', so, yeah. Congratulations. On your… tenacious… semen.

Sorry, what a fucking stupid thing to, listen you don't have to – I do have someone, in my life, his name is Mike, so you don't have to –

JOE. Can I…?

He gestures. She nods. He puts his hand on her belly. Holds it there.

TESS. If you're waiting for it to kick, don't bother. It's incredibly lazy.

JOE's phone rings. JOE takes his hand away. Checks the phone. Puts it away again.

You want to take that?

JOE. No. No, it's just Zhang Lin, / listen.

TESS. I don't mind. It's long-distance, you / should –

JOE. I said, don't worry about it, I'll call him back, listen, I would have said this anyway:

TESS. No, don't, / you don't have to –

JOE. I miss you. I can't stop – I think about you all the, so I mean, I know the timing is a little, and this guy, Mike, he sounds like a great – and I know I wasn't, that we met at a time when I was – but it's our lives isn't it, it's our lives so if there's any, even if you, you know, just for a coffee or something, even if there's the smallest, you know, a trace / of –

TESS. Joe –

JOE. I know.

TESS. Because –

JOE. I love you.

TESS. No.

JOE. No I know, I just had to. I just, I had to.

JOE kisses TESS. She lets him. Pulls away. TESS looks off.

TESS. I have to go. I have a meeting. I smell of milk. My mum says I should get used to that.

'

Did you ever find him?

'

JOE. He's dead, Tess.

,

JOE *puts his camera to his eye, takes her picture again.*
Pause.

You look so beautiful. You look exactly like I imagined you
would.

Scene Four

A gallery, Midtown Manhattan. Images of protest on the walls.
JOE*'s shot of the Tank Man. Next to a close-up of* TESS,
grinning, milk running down her face. Applause greets JOE *as*
he steps up to the microphone, clutching his notes.

JOE. I've spent a lot of time lately, apologising. For things I've
done. Not done. Things I've asked of other people. For
myself, in general, I guess. Which is, well, it's not an
unfamiliar feeling. So it's a pleasure for me to stand here in
front of you, and be able to say, well, just this: that these are
some pictures I've taken.

He glances behind him, gestures to the Tank Man
photograph. A tiny beat, then he looks back.

And of all the things I've done, I make no apology for them.

JOE *hesitates. Then folds his notes, nods, leaves the stage.*
Uncertain applause. MEL *approaches, wearing an eye*
patch. The men look at each other. Pleased to see each other,
but damned if they're going to say it. MEL *gestures to the*
Tank Man.

MEL. I know the guy who took that. He's kind of an asshole.

JOE. Hello, Mel.

MEL. And he can't write a speech for shit.

JOE. Yeah well, you aren't going to make any kind of
photographer. What happened?

MEL. Impertinent piece of Syrian shrapnel up and bit me.

JOE. Shit.

MEL (*pirate*). Oo-arr. You shoulda stuck around. Party got interesting after you left.

JOE. Is it – did you lose the eye?

MEL. Gotta socket like chopped liver. Wanna see? Scares the crap out of the kids.

JOE. No, I don't want to – what was that like?

MEL. Hurt like hell afterwards. Didn't know what hit me during. Moment before it happened I felt very alive. So anyway, I just came to see you in your splendour.

JOE. Well, thanks. It's pretty splendid, right?

BENNY *comes rushing up. Ignores* MEL, *shakes* JOE's *hand enthusiastically. Dressed in American sports-casual, and a pair of box-fresh Nike trainers.*

BENNY. Hey, man, I'm Benny. My uncle's a friend of yours, Zhang Lin? We were sposed to go to Peter Luger's!

JOE. Hey, yeah, yeah. Good to meet you.

MEL *is sloping off.*

You going? You don't want to stay for a drink or something?

MEL. Nah. My friends in the Automobile Association wouldn't like it.

JOE. Oh. Okay but, you didn't – I mean, what did you think, of the, of the exhibition?

'

MEL. I think. I think it's a hell of a store window, kid.

MEL *goes.* JOE *turns back to* BENNY.

JOE. I appreciate you coming down, I meant to call you but, I'm sorry about that night.

BENNY. Oh, man, don't even worry about it. Your girlfriend, ah, Tess? Very nice lady. She ate a thirty-two-ounce steak, no problem!

He puts up his hand for JOE *to high-five.*

JOE. Yeah, we broke up.

BENNY *takes his hand down. Gestures to the Tank Man picture.*

BENNY. Yeah so great picture, dude. Immense. So how much?

JOE. The gallery price them. I think that one's about eight thousand dollars.

BENNY. Okay, and is there any room for movement on that?

JOE. Sure. I could charge you nine thousand dollars.

,

BENNY. Look, dude, I never bought art before, I / don't know –

JOE. I'm sorry. That was. So you're studying at Harvard, right?

BENNY. I graduated last summer. I miss college, man, college was *awesome*! I work for this oil company now, they're like *the devil* but they helped me get a green card so I kind of have to stick it out for a while – hey! Ba!

ZHANG WEI *has entered, looking a little lost,* BENNY *waves to him.* ZHANG WEI *shakes* JOE's *hand, formal.*

You've met my dad, right?

JOE. *Yeah, uh nín hao ma?* [How are you?]

ZHANG WEI. *Hái hao.* [So so.] *Ní hao ma?*

JOE. *Hen hao.* [Very well.]

ZHANG WEI *hands* JOE *an iPod.* ZHANG WEI *speaks to* BENNY *in Mandarin. Gestures to* BENNY *to explain.*

BENNY. So Zhang Lin asked him to give you this. He wants you to listen to it. He says to tell you: 'I hope this story is big enough.'

ZHANG WEI *speaks very quickly in Mandarin.* JOE *tries to follow, looks to* BENNY.

JOE. My Mandarin is really – I'm sorry, what is he saying?

BENNY. He just, he says it's awesome to be here and, he's jetlagged, don't worry about it.

JOE. I'd like to know.

BENNY. Aw, man, this is super awkward.

He speaks to ZHANG WEI *in Mandarin, 'I asked you not to do this, Dad.' Turns to* JOE.

He says he is wondering what is wrong with you. He says his brother made guanxi with you. You took his hospitality and his gifts and his friendship and profited from them. When it was your turn you, like, failed him. He wanted your help and you didn't even return his phone calls. He is angry and disappointed. He said you're neither East nor West, which is, it's like a pretty bad insult. Shit, sorry, man.

ZHANG WEI *speaks in Mandarin again.*

He would also like me to say, what a wonderful exhibition. You are clearly a very talented man.

ZHANG WEI *nods his goodbye, and goes.*

Sorry, man. He's, like, I mean I like *love* him, but he can be kind of an asshole.

JOE. No, that's okay.

BENNY (*the Tank Man*). You know I think my dad knew him.

JOE. Yeah, well, your uncle said he did too.

BENNY. When I was growing up, I was the only kid at school who knew about 64. My dad had this tiny copy of this picture, and he used to get it out, sit on the floor by my bed with a candle and he'd go –

BENNY *laughs. Hands* JOE *a cigarette. Starts to roll one for himself.*

He'd point at the Tank Man and go: 'That little Dog-face! That little Dog-face nearly got me killed!'

JOE *looks up sharply.* BENNY *shakes his head, continues to roll his cigarette.*

At the time I just was like –

JOE. Dog-face?

BENNY. Yeah, it's a milk name, like a Chinese custom. Listen, so eight grand, that's totally cool, I mean it's an investment, right? It's like, enjoy your greenbacks while you can, dude. All gonna be yuan soon. We're coming for you, bitches!

JOE. What?

BENNY. It's a joke, man. Little… economics, like, joke –

JOE. Excuse me. I have to make a phone call.

JOE quickly moves away, impatient, takes out his phone. Dials, waits. Lights up on ZHANG LIN, in his Beijing apartment, as he answers his mobile. He is sitting, eating his breakfast.

Zhang Lin. It's Joe.

ZHANG LIN. I've been having some problems with my phone line.

JOE. Uh-uh, listen – I just saw Zhang Wei. And I met your nephew. Benny.

ZHANG LIN. Did Zhang Wei give you something?

JOE. Yeah. I haven't listened to it yet but. Does it say. What I think it's going to –

A PUBLIC SECURITY GUARD passes behind ZHANG LIN, searching his apartment. ZHANG LIN watches him.

ZHANG LIN. Yes, there's been some interference on the line. It's been causing me some trouble so our conversation may have to be quite… short. Do you understand me?

Joe?

ZHANG LIN takes a bite of food.

JOE. Yeah, Zhang Lin, I'm so. I'm / so –

ZHANG LIN. Your photograph made me look important.

I was frightened of it.

People looking at your picture, and seeing something.

And you try but you can't see what they see. Only what happened before, what happened after.

He was never me. Only a man who looked a bit like me.

And I wanted so much to look like him.

,

JOE. There's so much stuff I want to ask you.

ZHANG LIN. Yes. Another time, maybe? I have company.

,

JOE. What time is it there?

ZHANG LIN. Seven thirty. You're spoiling my breakfast.

JOE. Yeah? What you having?

ZHANG LIN. For breakfast?

JOE. Yeah.

ZHANG LIN. Crullers.

JOE. With congee?

ZHANG LIN. No, I hate congee. With soy milk.

The SECURITY GUARD *stands over* ZHANG LIN. *Holds his hand out.* ZHANG LIN *looks up at him.*

JOE. Sweet or salty?

ZHANG LIN dips his cruller in the milk. Takes a bite, still looking up at the GUARD.

ZHANG LIN. Sweet.

The GUARD *takes* ZHANG LIN's *phone from him. The line goes dead.* ZHANG LIN *wipes his mouth, picks up the possessions he has been allowed to take with him, in two carrier bags.*

JOE. Zhang Lin? Zhang Lin, hello?

Lights down on ZHANG LIN, *as he leaves his apartment, followed by the* GUARD, *a shopping bag in each hand. Hands shaking,* JOE *puts the earphones to the iPod in. Plays the track.*

ZHANG LIN (*voice-over*). The 1st of May. 1989.

> JOE *works the controls, impatient. The track fast-forwards.*
> JOE *stops, plays the recording. Sudden black. Chaos.*
> *Tiananmen Square, 1989. June 5th.* ZHANG LIN *enters.*
> *Bare-chested, blood-spattered, he holds his arms around*
> *himself. A* NURSE *runs on.*

NURSE. They've stopped firing, you should go home!

ZHANG LIN. Excuse me – that was – the woman, you just –
that's my wife. (*Louder.*) That's my wife. Please. That's my
wife.

NURSE. Where's your shirt?

ZHANG LIN (*thinks*). I ripped it up. For bandages.

NURSE. Wait there.

> *She runs off.* ZHANG LIN *shivers, he wipes his hand across*
> *his face, blood comes off, he stares at it. The* NURSE *runs*
> *on again, clutching an armful of things.*

Here, you can't go home like that.

> *She pulls a white shirt from the pile, gives it to him. He tries*
> *to thrust it back at her.*

ZHANG LIN. Whose is it? I don't want it.

NURSE. You want her things? It's just, her dress, bag. Shoes.
Jewellery, you'll want that.

> *She thrusts the items into* ZHANG LIN*'s arms, takes two*
> *carrier bags from her pocket, then kneels on the floor and*
> *puts* LIULI*'s things into the grocery bags.*

ZHANG LIN. What about. What about the body.

> *The* NURSE *shakes her head, kind.* ZHANG LIN
> *understands.*

NURSE. Will you be okay?

ZHANG LIN. I think. I think I'll take a walk.

> *The* NURSE *runs off. Moving slowly, automatically,* ZHANG
> LIN *pulls the white shirt on. Numbly picks up the bags.*

*Turns to us. Looking out, holding a grocery bag in each hand,
full of the last scraps of* LIULI. *We are looking, for the first
time, at a front view of the Tank Man.*

A lighting change. ZHANG LIN *walks, into the gallery. He
has reached the avenue.* ZHANG LIN *turns. His back, more
familiar view. The tanks approach.* ZHANG LIN *walks into
the tank's path.* ZHANG LIN's *movements are synchronised
with the projected, real film of the Tank Man.* JOE, *and we,
watch it with the knowledge of who this man is for the first
time. Of how he came to be there and what is in his bags.*

ZHANG LIN *turns to* JOE.

The two men look at one another.

Lights down.

www.nickhernbooks.co.uk

 facebook.com/nickhernbooks

 twitter.com/nickhernbooks